Policy Papers
in International Affairs

NUMBER 29

International Debt Threat

BARGAINING AMONG CREDITORS AND DEBTORS IN THE 1980S

Vinod K. Aggarwal

Institute of
International Studies

UNIVERSITY OF CALIFORNIA • BERKELEY

In sponsoring the Policy Papers in International Affairs series, the Institute of International Studies reasserts its commitment to a vigorous policy debate by providing a forum for innovative approaches to important policy issues. The views expressed in each paper are those of the author only, and publication in this series does not constitute endorsement by the Institute.

International Standard Book Number 0-87725-529-6

Library of Congress Catalog Card Number 87-80549

CONTENTS

APPENDIXES

CHRONOLOGIES OF DEBT RESCHEDULING NEGOTIATIONS

ACKNOWLEDGMENTS

An earlier version of this paper was sponsored by the Group of Thirty, New York. I owe a debt to many individuals. Om Aggarwal, Peggy Allen, Leslie Armijo, David Collier, Ernst Haas, Albert Fishlow, Robert Keohane, Gregory Luebbert, Jim Mahon, Guillermo O'Donnell, Robert Pringle, and Kenneth Waltz provided helpful comments on earlier drafts of this study. Special thanks are due to Ronald Gutfleish, who has worked on this project since its inception and whose contribution has been invaluable. Elizabeth Norville and David Platt ably provided research assistance and suggestions. For research support, I would like to thank the Rockefeller Foundation, and for its hospitality, the Brookings Institution. Many bankers and government officials agreed to provide me with insights on debt rescheduling issues but wished to remain anonymous. I remain solely responsible for the views expressed in this essay.

V.K.A.

The period from 1915 to 1935 has taught investors, bankers, and governmental authorities a valuable lesson. If the United States resumes the exportation of capital, in all likelihood it will be based on a sounder foundation than in the past, and many of the mistakes made in the post-war period will be avoided.

—John Madden, Marcus Nadler, and Harry Sauvain,
America's Experience as a Creditor Nation (1937)

[This book] tells of how little the investor has learned from the past experiences of earlier creditors, thus proving once again the truth of the Hegelian dictum that "We learn from history that we learn nothing from history."

—Max Winkler, *Foreign Bonds: An Autopsy* (1933)

1

INTRODUCTION

In the fall of 1982 it looked as if some of the major sovereign borrowers would be unable to continue servicing their enormous international debts. Unless they received extraordinary new financial aid, they would not be able to keep abreast of interest obligations, let alone amortize the principal on their loans, as debt-service requirements exceeded export receipts. Furthermore, it did not appear as if banks could coerce continued payments. They could not threaten to expropriate the assets of a sovereign debtor, as they could for a private one. Nor were banks, acting individually, able to restrict the debtors' access to capital in the future. Repudiation by any major debtor would have forced the banks to write off their loans, thereby decimating the capital of some of the largest banks.

Keynes's oft-quoted dictum, "If you owe the bank a thousand dollars, you have a problem; if you owe the bank a million dollars, the bank has a problem," seemed applicable indeed. With banks lacking any ostensible means of ensuring continued debt-servicing, it seemed that debtors had the upper hand.

The financial world faced dim prospects for engineering a solution to the crisis. Complicating the task of achieving collective action was the absence of any player willing to take a leadership role. The U.S. government, at least at the highest levels, intially favored a noninterventionist stance, as did many other OECD countries. Moreover, no single bank dominated the international financial market to the extent that it would be willing to bear the cost of organizing collective action alone. More than a thousand banks were involved on the creditor side—with a variety of objectives and fears.

Starting from such an apparently hopeless position, however, the banks, pushed by creditor governments and the International Monetary Fund (IMF), engineered a course of cooperation that has averted the worst of the scenarios for international financial collapse.

1

It appears as if the crisis has been successfully contained. The major debtors have rescheduled their loans with banks and official creditors, and most have agreed to follow adjustment policies suggested by the IMF. The banks, for their part, have had to put up new money and reschedule old loans, but at profitable rates. They have not had to write off a significant portion of what could have been bad debt, although the prices of their stocks have fallen significantly.

In this volume we will explain how banks, debtors, creditor governments, and international organizations managed to cooperate in heading off the crisis and examine the resulting costs and benefits from this effort. In particular, we will look at how the banks managed to develop a unified bargaining front, why the debtors failed to do so, and how governments and the IMF fostered a temporary resolution of the crisis. In doing so, we will review the constraints faced by various actors and analyze the bargaining strategies they used to overcome the obstacles in their way—both to achieve cooperation and to shift the distribution of costs and benefits in their favor.

This effort concentrates on the political dimension of the crisis. It does not attempt to evaluate the economic feasibility of these temporary solutions. Rather, it focuses on the bargaining process that led to the rescheduling arrangements and considers the political impediments to their continuation. The discussion is organized into five chapters.

Chapter 2 considers the static configuration of forces that would have come into play if the negotiations had been restricted to individual banks and debtors. Based on these factors alone, the prospects for reaching an agreement were slim. We explore several strategies in theory available to actors for improving their bargaining leverage to achieve a more equitable sharing of costs.

Chapter 3 begins with an examination of why the banks (particularly the large North American money-center banks) sought to develop a united front in dealing with debtors and the obstacles to cooperation that they faced. We then focus on their strategies to overcome these obstacles. The resulting interbank alliance proved to be a formidable force, capable of inducing a more cooperative response from debtors.

In Chapter 4 we review the impediments to forming a debtors' cartel. We will see why the large Latin American countries rejected a cartel (a proposal still being made by the smaller debtors) and instead sought to "go it alone."[1]

Chapter 5 analyzes the broader picture because the crisis has not been restricted to banks and debtor countries. Any breakdown in bank-debtor country relations would necessarily have repercussions elsewhere. Hence the 1982 crisis became a public affair with creditor governments and international organizations assuming prominent roles in its management.[2] We will see how banks tried to push a larger portion of the responsibility for providing new finance onto these participants. Furthermore, we will examine how the debtors sought support from creditor governments and international organizations in a partially successful effort to salvage repayment and adjustment programs that they could live with. The key role played by these outside actors has temporarily controlled the problem in a manner favorable to banks, albeit with minor concessions to debtors.

In conclusion Chapter 6 takes a look into the future. Although this potentially explosive crisis has been temporarily contained, it has not been defused. Adjustment has its price, particularly for debtor countries who have been undergoing painful periods of adjustment. If debtors become politically unstable as a result of economic hardships, it could spell doom for the rescheduling process that has been worked out thus far. Situational factors, broader goals, and the prospect of continuing interaction in the future present banks, creditor governments, international organizations, and debtor countries with a balance of incentives and obstacles that should allow a peaceful resolution to future crises. But if we are to avoid a breakdown of cooperation, it is imperative that creditor countries and international organizations take advantage of the current breathing space to accept a more active role in overseeing the terms of settlement among banks and debtors.

---

[1] Regarding the cartel, witness Peruvian President Alán García's inaugural address calling for a "united Latin America" to deal with the banks (*New York Times*, 29 July 1985).

[2] We will use the term "creditor government" to refer to both official creditors and the government of a country in which the international creditor banks are based. They are almost without exception one and the same.

A FRAMEWORK FOR ANALYZING NEGOTIATIONS: COOPERATION BETWEEN A BANK AND A DEBTOR

A crisis of confidence loomed foremost among the problems facing the banks and debtors in 1982. With Mexico, Brazil, Argentina, and Yugoslavia (among others) "on the brink of economic collapse,"[1] it was only natural that banks would want to cut credits to these and similar countries. Yet if banks simultaneously cut back on lending, it would make it more difficult for debtors to service their debts—thereby aggravating the situation for all actors.[2] Individual rationality could have led to collective irrationality. Gordon Richardson, Governor of the Bank of England, had this to say about the bankers' dilemma:

> Prudent banking practice may suggest that exposure should be reduced by the refusal of requests for new credits and the termination of existing lines or deposits as they mature; on the other hand, action of this sort, if precipitate or taken simultaneously by a number of the country's creditors, may well hasten and exacerbate the very difficulties from which the banks are trying to escape.[3]

The problem of simultaneous retrenchment was not unprecedented. In the early 1840s a wave of defaults was called on the debts of American states and the Bank of the United States as well.

---

[1]See Deputy Treasury Secretary R.T. McNamar's remarks before the Davos Symposium, Davos, Switzerland, 30 January 1984 (U.S. *Treasury Notes*).

[2]Just as Hungary and other Eastern bloc countries were "red-lined" following Poland's problems, Brazil fell victim to regional retrenchment by banks after the Mexican crisis. The whole Latin American region was seen as suspect, and banks quickly stopped lending.

[3]*Euromoney*, January 1983.

The Americans at first tried to continue raising credits in European markets to enable them to complete the public works projects necessary to generate the revenue for future debt service. But their efforts were rebuffed, and the capital had to be raised locally. Debt service was stopped for quite some time, and many European lenders suffered great losses. If European banks had continued the flow of credit, the disruption could have been avoided.[4]

With respect to the 1982 crisis, William Cline argued persuasively that the debtors were not insolvent but merely illiquid.[5] A cooperative effort that could help to ease these liquidity constraints could result in a more efficient outcome than debt moratoria and the resulting crises in international financial markets.

Cooperation, as opposed to mutual harmony, is not costless.[6] In cooperation, both parties must bear the brunt of the adjustment costs. For expository purposes we can envision four "ideal-typical" outcomes from negotiations over the distribution of costs:[7] (1) both the bank and debtor remain intractable, in which case the debtor repudiates its obligations and the bank stops lending; (2) the debtor holds firm by imposing a moratorium on repayment, while the bank keeps it liquid by providing a temporary inflow of capital; (3) the debtor acquiesces to bank demands for continued debt-servicing

---

[4]See Leland Jenks, *The Migration of British Capital to 1875* (New York: A.A. Knopf, 1927). For a comparison of past and current efforts to resolve debt crises, see Vinod K. Aggarwal, *Defusing the Debt Bomb: Conflict, Cooperation, and Costs in International Debt Rescheduling* (forthcoming).

[5]*International Debt and the Stability of the World Economy* (Washington, D.C.: Institute for International Economics, September 1983).

[6]The distinction between cooperation and mutual harmony comes from Robert Keohane, *After Hegemony* (Princeton: Princeton University Press, 1984). Keohane defines harmony as a situation where "each actor's policies (without regard for the interests of others) are regarded as facilitating the attainment of their goals" (p. 53).

[7]Although governments and international organizations were involved in debt reschedulings soon after debtors encountered problems in servicing their debt, I proceed with an obviously artificial construction to shed light on the factors influencing cooperation and costs in debt rescheduling and to illustrate how bargaining strategies influence outcomes. See the appendixes for a review of the involvement of different actors in the various reschedulings.

under increasing adjustment pain without receiving additional credits; and (4) the bank and debtor compromise by rescheduling the existing debt, new money is provided for the debtor, and the debtor follows adjustment policies designed to improve its ability to repay.

The above outcomes can be compared to a game of chicken. Both the bank and debtor would prefer to hold their ground and force the other to capitulate. For the debtor, outcome 2 is optimal, whereas outcome 3 would be best for the bank. Each has the same second choice (4), where both bear some portion of the adjustment burden. That outcome is in turn preferable to shouldering the brunt of the adjustment burden alone. The banks claim that the worst outcome for each would be mutual intransigence (1), leading to the collapse of the international financial system.

Debtors generally fear such a breakdown, not merely because they may be cut off from access to future capital, but also because their trade, which is in most cases essential for short-run survival, would grind to a halt. For instance, when banks extended about $300 million in trade credits to Peru in 1985, one New York banker warned, "If they get too confrontational, we'll cut off all that. Then they won't be able to import food or spare parts, and there'll be an immediate political cost."[8] This fear is reflected in Peru's efforts to stay current on the servicing of its trade financing—even though it has linked general debt repayments to its export growth.

A stalemate is clearly the least preferable outcome and could create a crisis situation for the banks. However, it is not so obvious that the debtors hold the same to be true; moreover, it is unlikely they would publicly admit their fears of breakdown. They may feel that they could survive even without bank funds and be better off in doing so than being forced to adjust their economies under IMF strictures.[9] If the debtors can convince the banks that they would rather have the financial system collapse than be forced to adjust, an effective strategy for them may be to bluff.[10] In that case, the

[8]*New York Times*, 30 July 1985.

[9]See Anatole Kaletsky, *The Costs of Default* (New York: Priority Press Publications, 1985) for an argument that debtors may be better off repudiating their debt instead of submitting to harsh adjustment programs.

[10]In technical terms, "called bluff" is where one actor is in a prisoner's dilemma situation, while the other faces the payoffs for a game of "chicken."

banks might have to capitulate rather than risk systemic collapse. Argentina has at times adopted such a position, as is illustrated by the following threat, issued by its ambassador to the Latin American common market:

> It is good for my country to be so isolated. . . . We can go to East Germany, Bulgaria, Hungary. If we are pushed to buy more imports from the Soviet Union, we will and it won't be our fault. . . . Frankly, no one will tell you the government is making contingency plans. But they are.[11]

In sum, by holding firm in this admittedly artificially constructed static game, it appears that the debtor can make individual banks accede to its demands. The following look at the configuration of interests and capabilities conditioning the negotiations would seem to support such a view.

In the rest of this chapter we will focus on the options available to banks and debtors acting individually. In later chapters we will see how banks improved their position by allying among themselves and with other actors.

THE SETTING FOR NEGOTIATIONS

Three factors shape the prospects for banks and debtors (as well as other actors) to reach a cooperative agreement. These same factors also provide insight into the likely distribution of costs and benefits. These are as follows: (1) whether actors are organized in an anarchical or hierarchical manner; (2) the type of functional similarity or differentiation among units; and (3) the amount and distribution of material and informational capabilities in their possession.[12]

Anarchy/Hierarchy. Both the banks and debtors would prefer compromise to stalemate. But their mutual interest will be realized only through an agreement that will work against cheating. In the

[11] *Wall Street Journal*, 26 June 1984.

[12] Kenneth Waltz, *Theory of World Politics* (Reading, Mass.: Addison-Wesley, 1979), looks at how these factors influence international stability. He does not, however, consider the *amount* of capabilities in his systemic analysis, but only their distribution.

international private credit market there is no overarching authority which can ensure that a bank and debtor country will abide by their agreements. A cooperative agreement is not stable. At any time, knowing that the other's worst fear is mutual intransigence, one of the two may resort to brinksmanship to win more lucrative terms.

Functional Similarity/Differentiation. Debtors seek continued access to large sums of development and trade financing, and banks are the only institutions capable of mobilizing these. In a crisis situation, this functional dissimilarity can lead to a divergence in their interests. The banks, for example, may be pressed by stockholders to show large profits each quarter (particularly in the United States). This objective may conflict with a longer-run interest of keeping the debtors liquid until they develop the capacity to pay off their obligations.

The two groups are by no means homogeneous entities. Below we will see how differences within these groups affected the ability of both the banks and debtors to achieve united bargaining fronts. For instance, larger money-center banks are much more heavily involved than regional banks in lending to sovereign debtors, creating different propensities to contribute additional funds to debtors. In another vein, certain debtors may feel a greater obligation to respond to the exigencies of domestic politics than others. They may be pressed to take a more confrontational stand toward the banks, even though their leaders, fearing a head-on collision, would prefer compromise.

Material and Informational Capabilities. The amount and distribution of actor capabilities in a variety of areas also influence outcomes. In the long run, it is only through commercial banks, and not through official creditors, that developing countries can obtain the large amounts of capital necessary to finance continued industrialization (without becoming what they consider to be overreliant on direct foreign investment). But certain debtors may feel that they are no longer in need of bank assistance. As the *Financial Times* noted,

> Unlike most other Latin American countries, Argentina can demonstrate the ability to pay off a substantial portion of its $39 billion foreign debt. It is almost self-sufficient in energy,

and enjoys a food surplus as well as considerable established industrial capacity. . . . These advantages have also brought home to Argentines the knowledge that theirs is one of the few countries that could survive for any length of time a repudiation of foreign debt. . . . Argentina does not need to be active in foreign trade.[13]

If the banks act individually in imposing sanctions for delinquent payments, debtors can threaten to turn to more cooperative lenders. Individual debtors have a clear advantage in such a situation.

The amount of information on a debtor's economic status and the ease with which it can be obtained affect the willingness of banks to cooperate. In an information-rich environment, actors might be more willing to trust each other since they are better able to gauge each others' motivation. At the outset of the debt reschedulings, given the large number of banks involved in lending to sovereign countries, it was difficult to keep track of the debtors' true financial positions.[14]

The distribution of information is crucial as well. Individual banks often know precious little about a country's economic situation. Indeed one observer claimed that "Frugal middle class Americans would have to give more information to their friendly neighborhood bank to get a car loan than Poland gave to develop a country."[15]

Considering the static situation described so far, it would be unlikely that banks and debtors could reach agreement. Neither can ensure that the other will abide by any proposed agreement, and the functional dissimilarity of these actors creates sharp conflicts of interest. If there was to be an agreement, it would be unstable and would clearly favor the debtors because of capability differences in the debtors' favor. Although this static situation outlines the initial constraints faced by actors, the actors can expand the scope of the negotiations in an effort to improve their position.

[13] 4 November 1983.

[14] The creation of the Institute for International Finance in 1983 as an information clearing house for international banks can be seen as an effort to address this lack of information.

[15] *Wall Street Journal*, 8 August 1981.

BARGAINING STRATEGIES

Several strategies can be used by banks and debtors to promote conciliation and to shift the distribution of costs and benefits in their favor. These include a recourse to norms and rules, to one's own capabilities, through links to the future, and to both state and non-state allies.[16]

Recourse to Norms and Rules. The least expensive course that actors may take is to refer to norms and rules applying to the topic under negotiation. For example, during the 1982 crisis the banks sought to keep the negotiations along the same lines discussed by Charles Lipson:

> The debt negotiations themselves are now routinized. The debtor approaches the IMF or a major creditor seeking to reorganize its debt. As the IMF negotiates its standby agreement, private and official creditors conduct their separate meetings . . . which presuppose an IMF standby arrangement. . . . These ad hoc conferences are convened at the creditors' discretion and conform to the creditors' position that debt relief is an extreme event, forced by traumatic circumstances . . . best handled by short-term, generally non-concessionary, debt reorganization.[17]

The rescheduling efforts of 1982-84 conformed to this pattern. However, there was a difference in magnitude, the Mexican bailout being labeled "unprecedented" and "historic" by the participants at the highest levels.[18] The Mexican government was forced to go

---

[16]For a detailed discussion of bargaining, see Vinod K. Aggarwal and Pierre Allan, "Evolution in Bargaining Theories: Toward an Integrated Approach to Explain Strategies of the Weak"; paper presented at the American Political Science Association meetings, Chicago, September 1983.

[17]"The International Organization of Third World Debt," *International Organization* 35, 4 (1981):519-20.

[18]Federal Reserve Chairman Paul Volker referred to the crisis as "unprecedented." To IMF Managing Director Jacques de Larosière it was "historic." William Rhodes of Citibank spoke of the leaders of the commercial banks as "pioneers." Whether the situation was indeed unprecedented is open to dispute. Commercial banks came together to aid government debtors in the 1920s, leading up to the Hoover Moratorium in June 1931. During this period central

immediately to the U.S. government for emergency relief. Outside actors played a more prominent role, particularly in forcing reluctant banks to cooperate.

Debtors can also appeal to precedent, as Alfonso Celso Pastore, President of the Brazilian Central Bank noted: "It's like a Formula One Race. We're letting Mexico take the lead and we're going to ride in its slipstream, later overtaking them to achieve even better repayment conditions."[19]

Negotiators realize that current policies may establish a pattern for future interaction. The IMF and the commercial banks were afraid of making concessions for fear of setting an undesirable precedent. In response to suggestions that interest owed by the debtors be automatically capitalized, one banker remarked as follows: "Everybody gets the same terms if you have interest capitalization, making it difficult to discriminate as we currently do with jumbo loans."[20]

Recourse to Capabilities. Negotiators may ignore norms and rules and instead use their various power capabilities in pushing for more favorable terms. These capabilities can be either specific to the issue being negotiated (e.g., the financial resources of a bank) or from some other, possibly linked, issues (e.g., a debtor may link trade liberalization to continued debt-servicing). Using threats and links is a more costly approach than appealing to standard operating rules and procedures—in part because of the high degree of uncertainty associated with their use. Hence if a bank threatens to cut off future finance, a debtor may call its bluff. Linking outside issues may increase the number of participants in the negotiations, which could lead to unforeseen complications. Though increasing the number of

banks were particularly active, as well as some commercial banks, most notably J.P. Morgan and Company, in putting together rescheduling packages for problem European debtors. See Charles Kindleberger, *Manias, Panics, and Crashes* (New York: Basic Books, 1978); Stephen V.O. Clarke, *Central Bank Cooperation, 1924-31* (New York: Federal Reserve Bank of New York, 1967); and Albert Fishlow, "Lessons from the Past," *International Organization* 39, 3 (Summer 1985).

[19]*New York Times*, 23 September 1984.

[20]Interview with French banker. Interest capitalization is an automatic conversion of interest due into principal.

issues in the negotiations may make cooperation more difficult,[21] it might also make it possible for negotiators to make side payments in order to reach a compromise. This factor has been critical in promoting interbank alliances.

Links to the Future. Because the actors are not engaged in a single-play game, the purely static situation changes. Banks and debtors expect to interact with each other in the future. The iterative nature of their interaction has two major effects on their bargaining relations: it introduces a solution to the problem of establishing binding agreements, and it evens up the distribution of capabilities in bargaining.

We saw that the anarchical situation, in which banks and debtors find themselves, results in an inability to trust each other and negotiate binding arrangements. But if they will be interacting over time, an incentive to cooperate presents itself. Those who abide by contractual agreements establish good reputations and can reduce the price of "risk premiums" in future negotiations. Furthermore, banks and debtors now have the opportunity to reciprocate for cooperative behavior. They can play "tit-for-tat"—responding in kind to actions made in good faith by the other side. Following this logic, in early 1985 Mexico decided to pay part of the principal it owed on its debt to encourage a cooperative response from the banks on its proposal for a multi-year rescheduling. Banks and debtors interact in more issues than just in the rescheduling of debts. Their relations in the larger arena also affect the establishment of reputation. By increasing the number of "observation points," actors are able to judge whether their opponents are trustworthy, which may increase the chances that the latter will cooperate with others. In addition, other things being equal, the larger the number of issues on which particular actors interact and cooperate, the higher the probability that they will perceive the relationship as valuable. Hence they will be wary of a precipitous action that may undermine this relationship.

Links to future interaction shift the distribution of costs and benefits in favor of the banks. Banks are able to restrict the extension of further credits, which (as we noted above) are a virtual

[21]See Robert Axelrod, *Conflict of Interest* (Chicago: Markham, 1970), ch. 2.

requisite for trading in the international marketplace. Of course the banks must band together for any such threat to be credible.

The possibility that banks may be capable of cooperating in this manner distinguishes the current crisis from waves of defaults which occurred in the 1820s and 1890s. In those crises the sovereign debt was generally held by individual bondholders and not the banks (who were responsible for placing the issues with the public). Individual bondholders were powerless to cut off future credits to delinquent debtors insofar as there was a willing merchant banking house ready to market their debt once again.[22] The British Council of Foreign Bondholders was formed in 1868 as part of an attempt to cut these debtors off from the market. However, this effort was relatively ineffective in preventing default as the French and German governments would not allow it to operate in their markets.[23]

Recourse to Allies. Banks and debtors may seek either state or nonstate allies to increase their bargaining leverage. Banks in particular need help from other banks. Individual banks rarely have complete and accurate information on the financial status of debtor countries, and (as we argued above) cannot successfully impose sanctions on an individual basis.

Debtors may also seek to band together to increase the costs that the banks will have to bear if they do not provide them with additional liquidity. In addition, banks and debtors may compete for the favor of creditor governments who can provide information about and exert leverage over both groups. The banks may seek help from international organizations to provide them with information on the total debt levels of both individual banks and individual debtors, to draw up adjustment plans, and to monitor the economic performance of debtors.

We noted above that it was unlikely that banks and debtors would come to terms. If an agreement was concluded, it would favor debtors over individual banks, who are unable to threaten

[22]The London Stock Exchange maintained a rule to refuse quotes to a government in default on its loans (Jenks, p. 284).

[23]See Fishlow for an insightful analysis of these crises. Also see Aggarwal (forthcoming).

effective retribution. Yet we have now seen that there are bargaining strategies that might promote compromise and force the debtors to share the costs. In particular, alliances provide an important source of bargaining leverage. As the 1982 crisis was likely to expand into other arenas, outside actors were motivated to secure cooperative solutions. The banks and debtors then played on these interests to develop broader alliances and increase their bargaining leverage, to the point where most costs were shifted onto the debtors' shoulders.[24]

[24]These costs will be discussed in Chapter 5 below.

3

COOPERATION AMONG BANKS

The discussion in Chapter 2 focusing on bargaining between a debtor and an individual bank served a heuristic purpose in explaining how we will analyze the rescheduling efforts. But banks and debtors rarely—if ever—interact on a one-to-one basis.

We saw that a bank's threat to cut off a debtor's access to capital has little credibility if debtors can simply turn to other, more willing banks for loans. To avoid being played off against each other by debtors, banks must develop and maintain a unified front.

From the start of the 1982 crisis, lead banks were aware of the need to take a united position vis-à-vis debtors. The banks were confronted with the twin problems of negotiating the terms of rescheduling with debtors and reaching an agreement on how the burden was to be distributed among themselves. The resolution of these issues was complicated by the overwhelming differences in the banks' exposures. To cope with these problems larger banks drew upon their capabilities, used novel organizational forms, and sought alliances with creditor countries, international organizations, and even debtors in their effort to raise jumbo loans.

In this section, we will first look at the various obstacles to interbank cooperation before turning to an examination of linkage strategies banks employed to overcome these constraints. Chapter 4 will analyze how debtors attempted to handle the same problems.

OBSTACLES TO COOPERATION

In negotiating with debtors and apportioning among themselves the burden of providing new financing, banks require some means of enforcing collective action. Heavily exposed banks want to see continued credit flows to debtor countries—as long as these enable them to keep current on their obligations. However, individual banks would like to let the responsibility for these actions fall on others. Unfortunately for them, they are unable to invoke legal sanctions against banks refusing to contribute to the collective effort.

The problems encountered in raising money for Project Four, one part of the 1983 Brazilian rescheduling arrangement (restoring interbank loans), illustrate the difficulties that banks faced. When the banks came up $3 billion short of their original $9 billion target, the lead banks could not turn to any legal authority to force recalcitrant banks to come up with additional money. Instead the larger banks contributed more than their shares. If such a pattern were to continue, the larger banks would bear a disproportionate share of the costs of rescheduling. As we will see below, the big banks were able to use linkage strategies to improve their position.

The situation was very complex owing to the number of actors involved in the rescheduling arrangements. About 600 banks were involved in the 1983 Mexican rescheduling and 560 in the Brazilian agreement. The "free rider" syndrome becomes most pronounced in such big groups, where communication is difficult and cheating easy. As the number of actors increases with a greater dispersion of these capabilities, it becomes more difficult to work out cooperative agreements. In addition, larger groups are more likely than smaller ones to contain divergent interests.

The resolution of these issues was further complicated by the sharp differences in the banks' exposures—particularly between money-center and regional or smaller banks. Bank exposure may vary by capital outlay, timing, maturity, type of loan, or type of borrower. The more vulnerable a bank was, the more inclined it would be to extend new finance in an effort to keep problem loans from becoming nonperforming assets. Clearly not all banks were in the same position in this respect. To a large extent, the relative commitment of banks tended to vary by nationality—a factor influencing interests and participation of different governments.

On the whole, European banks were less heavily committed in Latin America than their North American counterparts, whose financial situation could be either salvaged or decimated by the actions of a single debtor.[1] For instance, Citicorp earned more than

[1]British bank loans were only a little more than their combined equity,

25 percent of its gross profits in 1983 as a result of interest payments made possible by the Brazilian jumbo loan, and thus it was bound to show a greater interest in keeping up the flow of credit than banks with less at stake. In Latin America the U.S. banks had a hard time getting other banks to go along with what the Europeans criticized as an "American show." In Poland, on the other hand, European banks were much more exposed than the American ones.[2] Here it was they who feared that "one single bank might break ranks, declare a default and send the whole edifice of Poland's debt tottering in ruins."[3]

Exposures were skewed within national boundaries as well. North American banks accounted for 35.7 percent of total international lending to Argentina, Brazil, and Mexico. However, nine banks in the United States were responsible for three fifths of this total; one fifth was accounted for by the next fifteen banks, and only one fifth by all the rest. This imbalance fostered continued conflict between this last group of less exposed smaller banks (whose lending to these countries averaged 43.9 percent of their capital in 1982) and the more heavily exposed money-center banks (with an average exposure of 112.5 percent).[4]

These differences proved crucial in paving the way for an oligopolistic domination of the rescheduling process. The banks with the largest stakes took the lead from the start and then tried to dictate the terms to their smaller brethren. Yet the smaller banks did not always fall into line. Since they were less exposed, they were less willing to contribute more funds to problem debtors. As an

Swiss and German bank loans about half that level, and large North American bank loans accounted for over twice as much. See Paolo Nogueira-Batista, Jr., "International Debt Reschedulings since mid-1982: Rescue Operations and Their Implications for Commercial Banks and Debtor Countries"; UNCTAD Doc. MFD/TA/30 (September 1984).

[2]The U.S. share of Poland's commercial bank debt dropped to 8 percent in 1981 from 25 percent in 1976 (*Wall Street Journal*, 21 December 1981).

[3]*Financial Times*, 22 June 1981.

[4]Manufacturers Hanover Trust led the way with an exposure equal to 200.3 percent of its capital (from Richard Dale and Richard Mattione, *Managing Global Debt* [Washington, D.C.: The Brookings Institution, 1983], p. 14), and Batista, p. 20.

official at the National Bank of Detroit commented about the ongoing negotiations with Argentina, "On balance, the smaller banks couldn't care less. Almost without exception, Argentina has been making interest payments of less than $20,000."[5]

Other differences arose among banks about the basis date to be used in determining how much each bank should contribute to new loans. Since the French had greatly increased their exposure to Brazil during 1982-83, they wanted to use an early basis date to minimize their total contribution to the Brazilian jumbo loan, a move which the Americans opposed.[6]

The maturity and type of outstanding loans also varied among banks, which in turn affected their ability to agree among themselves on the terms of debt refinancing. Japanese banks were dismayed when they learned that expected contributions to the Brazilian jumbo loan had been calculated on the basis of outstanding medium- and long-term loans. American banks had more short-term loans outstanding, so the Japanese were being asked to contribute a relatively higher proportion of total exposure. In the 1982 Mexican agreement, the Swiss objected to the inclusion of bonds in determining their total exposure. Sometimes banks that participated in relatively secure trade credit loans found these being lumped together with other loans. As one regional banker complained, "We don't like seeing our short-term trade loans becoming longer term loans."[7]

Conflicts of interest erupted over how to treat different borrowers. In particular, the differences between private and public loans spurred a sharp division. Since some banks had more prudently lent to government agencies at lower spreads, they felt penalized by accords which lumped riskier private and public loans together.[8]

Information constraints played a key role in bank cooperation. The banks found themselves in the unenviable position of having little information about the debtors' economic positions. The *Wall Street Journal* recounts the following story:

[5]*New York Times*, 28 March 1984.

[6]Interviews with French bankers.

[7]*New York Times*, 12 April 1984, p. 29.

[8]Interviews with bankers in Europe.

Early [in the autumn of 1982], several top Brazilian officials paid a call on executives of an international bank that had lent money to Brazil. Over lunch the officials disclosed that a big part of Brazil's international reserves consisted of uncollectable debts owed by Poland.

How did the chairman of the bank react? "You mean before or after I fainted?" he asked.

"The liquidity we thought was there wasn't there," one of his aides [added].[9]

Variations in the *distribution* of information posed a problem as well. As regional banks lacked large staffs abroad, they followed the advice of the money-center banks in joining loan syndicates. But when the rescheduling agreements were being worked out, they complained that they were being left in the dark. Some regional bankers even claimed that they had to rely on the press to find out what was going on. Furthermore, as one banker commented about the regional banks, "There are obviously some 'Johnny come lately's' who went in late without adequate staff and did not understand and are now having a difficult time."[10]

The functional similarity of banks—the fact that they constitute a community with similar values—generates shared norms of behavior to which individual banks feel they must conform. This socialization process has its bad and good points. On the negative side, banks tend to follow each other and lend more and more to the same countries without developing a complete picture of the countries' total debts. In 1980 one American banker noted, "Maybe no one's making a fortune here any longer, but you've got to be in Mexico. This is where the action is."[11] Moreover, the banks also stop their lending in unison. As Dale and Mattione have commented,

The credit standing of a country in debt to a large number of lenders does not so much depend on each lender's view of the country's prospects as it does on each lender's assessment of how other lenders may react to adverse developments elsewhere.[12]

[9]30 August 1983.

[10]*Financial Times*, 21 December 1982, p. 8.

[11]*Institutional Investor*, December 1980, p. 158.

[12]P. 24.

On the positive side, this socialization acts to prevent banks from free-riding at the expense of other banks and encourages them to cooperate with one another.

Aside from their similar functions, banks exist in different institutional environments. Nationalized French banks need not worry about showing a quarterly profit and can take a longer-run view of profitability. Swiss banks, which have to declare profits only on an annual basis, are also more willing to take a somewhat longer-run view than the Americans. This different regulatory treatment by national authorities necessarily affects priorities. The Europeans make greater provisions for losses from international loans—in part owing to a more favorable tax treatment of these reserves and in part because of pressure from regulatory authorities. In West Germany, for instance, provisioning against doubtful assets significantly reduces tax liabilities. The Swiss central bank has encouraged extra provisioning against loans to Mexico, Brazil, and Poland.[13]

National regulatory differences also come into play over the issue of interest capitalization. The European banks in particular have been suggesting that they should capitalize interest payments instead of extending new capital. In contrast, North American banks, which have to write off loans as nonperforming if interest payments are delayed, oppose such a plan.

Differing foreign policy objectives among countries can make it difficult for banks to cooperate with one another. In the Polish crisis, the West German government was interested in maintaining ties with Poland and therefore wished to encourage liberal rescheduling arrangements. By contrast, Defense Secretary Caspar Weinberger encouraged U.S. bankers to declare Poland in default, an effort which the bankers resisted.[14] In the case of Argentina, the British government's antagonism toward the Argentines led it to stall rescheduling talks in late summer 1982, as bankers would not extend new loans until Britain released $1.45 billion in frozen assets.[15] U.S. Deputy Treasury Secretary McNamar was then forced to shuttle between the British and Argentine delegations at the

[13] Batista, p. 25.

[14] *Los Angeles Times*, 4 July 1982.

[15] *Business Week*, 13 September 1982.

annual IMF meetings in Toronto before the sanctions were lifted on 15 September.[16]

What has this analysis led us to expect? It appears that the larger banks would be motivated to band together—in Latin America under American leadership and in Poland under West German leadership—due to their highly exposed positions. Moreover, the relatively small number of large banks would facilitate the making and keeping of agreements, as would the high degree of functional similarity among them. On the whole, banks of relatively equal size and comparably high exposures should be willing to share the costs of rescheduling more or less equally.

By contrast, we would expect smaller and regional banks to be highly resistant to any accord, and larger banks might end up bearing most of the costs of providing new financing to debtors. As we will see below, however, the strategies of lead banks increased the participation of smaller banks and allowed larger banks to shift the refinancing burden onto these smaller banks.

OVERCOMING THE OBSTACLES TO BARGAINING

COOPERATION AMONG LARGE BANKS

The large banks needed to establish a united position before confronting the smaller regionals. Without such a position, the threat of sanctions for noncooperative behavior would have little credibility. The oligopolistic nature of the banking community and the acute overexposure of large banks facilitated cooperation. Nonetheless, although they had developed some procedures to deal with debtor countries in financial binds, banks had never put together a jumbo loan of the magnitude required for Mexico in 1982.[17]

As in any case of bargaining among equal powers, an equitable outcome is likely, but the production of public goods is made more

[16]Darrell Delamaide, *Debt Shock* (Garden City, N.Y.: Doubleday, 1984), p. 115.

[17]Although later reschedulings involving Brazil and Argentina (among others) were difficult, the large banks interested in promoting cooperation could and did appeal to the Mexican precedent to foster cooperation among banks.

difficult. Individual banks of equal power will have little incentive to pay for the complicated process of rescheduling loans if their costs exceed the total benefits that they will derive. But if there are a small number of large creditors with a large stake, they may be more willing and able to make sacrifices to work out a debt rescheduling.[18]

In the Latin American crises (as noted), the large U.S. banks took the lead. They put pressure on the European banks, using the crisis atmosphere to their advantage to force quick agreement. Although these tactics raised protests from some large banks (one Swiss banker complained about being treated as a "satellite"),[19] the Europeans on the whole accepted the need to follow the American lead. Indeed one French banker, after complaining half-heartedly about Citibank "imperialism," remarked that it would be "nonsense to try to increase French influence [for four reasons:] the bigger commitment by U.S. banks; [the fact that U.S. banks] had lead managed the loans, they are respected the world over, and they got organized quickly."[20]

Two other factors facilitated coordination among the larger banks. First, representatives of large banks in both Britain and France meet frequently. The British clearing banks (with the blessing of the Bank of England) have met regularly since 1982 in the Sovereign Credit Risk Committee.[21] The French set up a committee of the top seven banks to maintain close contact with the Treasury, and to keep

---

[18]On the whole, it would appear that exposure is more important than size in determining the willingness of banks to cooperate in reschedulings. For example, First Wisconsin National Bank, a regional, was willing to go along with restructuring plans in 1982-84 because it had large Latin American loans outstanding relative to its size (see *New York Times*, 12 April 1984, p. 29). At the same time, a banker from a large U.S. bank remarked that "While applauding the IMF's role in Mexico and Brazil, [the bank] would not comply with similar requests to go on lending to eastern Europe, where it is relatively less exposed" (Group of Thirty, *Commercial Banks and the Restructuring of Cross-Border Debt* [New York, 1983], p. 13).

[19]Interview with Swiss commercial banker.

[20]Interview with French commercial banker.

[21]Interviews with British commercial bankers.

everyone apprised of developments during the 1982 crisis.[22] Second, both the British and French banks have led advisory groups in re-scheduling African debt.[23] In this connection, large banks realize that they will be interacting with each other in the future—even as regional and smaller banks retrench from international lending. Recalcitrant banks are likely to develop a bad reputation that will impair future business.

In sum, large banks overcame obstacles to cooperation relatively easily. But they still faced the problem of ensuring that smaller banks would participate. This obstacle proved more difficult to surmount.

ENSURING PARTICIPATION BY SMALLER BANKS

The smaller banks were not eager to contribute new funds. As one regional banker angrily suggested to the large banks leading the rescheduling effort, "You've bailed them out, but why should we bail you out?"[24]

Big banks, however, can use the four strategies noted in Chapter 2 to foster cooperation—i.e., norms and rules, capabilities, links to the future, and recourse to allies. With respect to capabilities, big banks acting together can at times simply impose agreements on smaller banks. Large creditors do have coercive power. In inter-national banking, only lending syndicates can declare a default, and to do so generally requires a two-thirds vote.[25] Because voting is determined by each bank's share of the total overall loan, large lenders can stave off such a declaration. Smaller creditors are left with the choice of ratifying (which involves contributing new credit) or refusing to abide by the syndicate agreement. A bank choosing the

[22]Interview with French commercial banker.

[23]See Batista; also see Charles Lipson, "Bankers' Dilemma: Private Coopera-tion in Rescheduling Sovereign Debts," *World Politics* (October 1985), for a discussion of cooperation among banks.

[24]*Fortune*, 11 July 1983, p. 52.

[25]In the more recent Mexico rescheduling of 1984, 55 percent of banks can declare Mexico in default if they feel it has failed to comply with its economic targets.

second option is threatened by exclusion from future syndicated loans.[26]

In more benevolent fashion, the larger banks might use their greater overall resources to provide side payments to the smaller banks in exchange for their cooperation. They could buy some of the outstanding LDC loans of banks that agree to cooperate in jumbo loans. Such actions are comparatively rare since the money-center banks fear that these would set a precedent and encourage other smaller banks to seek similar arrangements.

With respect to links to the future, banks do not bargain with each other over rescheduling in isolation. They are influenced by other ties having to do with domestic loan-making, correspondent relationships, and so on. Hence smaller banks will be reluctant to jeopardize their long-term relationship with larger banks. As one observer remarked,

> We ... doubt that any U.S. bank is likely to break ranks and try to foreclose. . . . A small bank, especially, has to have access to the world money market and big customers; a reputation for being a solo artist is not considered desirable.[27]

Although they can exert substantial power, large banks have still ended up contributing more than their proportional shares to financing arrangements. Only 121 of more than 500 banks were asked to contribute to the 1983 Brazilian jumbo loan.[28] Later in Project Four of this effort, regional banks refused to participate fully in restoring interbank lines. Although the money-center banks (particularly Citibank and Morgan Guaranty) contributed more than their shares, the regionals refused to help out.[29]

If the large banks hoped to maintain a degree of interbank cooperation, they needed to use more than their capabilities and

[26]Interviews. Also see Charles Lipson, "International Debt and International Institutions," in *International Debt*, ed. Miles Kahler (Ithaca: Cornell University Press, 1986).

[27]*Wall Street Journal*, 13 April 1984.

[28]*Wall Street Journal*, 30 August 1983.

[29]Particularly deficient were the National Bank of Detroit, Wells Fargo, and the Bank of New York (*Fortune*, 11 July 1983, p. 53, and *Wall Street Journal*, 30 August 1983).

appeals to their close connections. To create a greater degree of hierarchy among themselves and increase their coercive power, the large money-center banks followed two important strategies: they developed innovative organizational forms, and they sought international organizations, debtors, and creditor governments as allies.

Faced with difficulties in coercing smaller banks to support their rescheduling agreements with debtor countries, the large banks chose to divide the large collection of banks from which they sought contributions into smaller groups. This strategy stemmed from the long experience they had in syndicating large loans to smaller banks.

In the Mexican negotiations, an advisory committee of fourteen major banks was organized as a focal point for discussions.[30] Each U.S. member of the committee took responsibility for gaining the support of ten different regional banks. In turn, each regional bank took responsibility for ten smaller banks in its area. In similar fashion, banks outside the United States assumed responsibility for banks in their geographical regions. Several subcommittees were set up to deal with specific problems, such as Mexico's macroeconomic situation, defining types of debt, and managing interbank lines.[31]

In the 1983 Brazil rescheduling, the same pattern prevailed. Antonio Gebauer of Morgan Guaranty took the lead as conflicting positions immobilized Citibank, Brazil's largest creditor.[32] When Gebauer formed the advisory groups in charge of different aspects of the rescheduling, no regional banks were involved. Without representation, they were even more reluctant to cooperate with the larger banks and let their interbank lines drop—leading to the collapse of what was known as Phase I. When William Rhodes of Citibank took over as chairman of the committee to advise Brazil, he followed a strategy similar to the one he had pursued in Mexico. Regional banks were given a role in encouraging recalcitrant banks to come up with their shares in the rescheduling. As a result, the large banks had more success in enlisting their cooperation.

[30]This approach has since become the standard operating procedure for dealing with troubled debtor countries.

[31]Joseph Kraft, *The Mexican Rescue* (New York: Group of Thirty, 1984) and interviews with bankers.

[32]The following discussion draws on *Fortune*, 11 July 1983.

These strategies facilitated cooperation in several ways. First, by bringing banks together in an organized fashion, they increased the amount of information available to banks. In addition, the close contact generated among banks by the development of many small groups served to increase the degree of trust members had in each other. Furthermore, such an arrangement reduced the costs of monitoring shirkers who were unwilling to contribute their shares.

Organizational innovation served to increase overall material capabilities as well. By developing a close-knit organization, banks were better able to raise large amount of capital in a shorter period of time. Within these smaller, regionally concentrated groupings, smaller institutions generally had many ties (a correspondent banking relationship and participation in syndicated loans) with the key bank. Consequently large banks had an easier time in generating support for the rescheduling agreements.

Systematic decentralization also promotes a degree of informal hierarchy among the banks. Although there are no formal rules and sanctions connected to noncompliance, the enhanced ability to monitor cooperation, combined with the greater similarity among group members, increased the pressure on recalcitrant banks. Such banks are likely to have a greater density of interaction with other members—both on the number of issues and over time. This creation of a "parish" provides a purely rational reason to cooperate.[33] Even if deviant banks are not swayed by social pressure, others may well be. Their reluctance to cooperate with the deviant in the future provides a strong incentive for all to conform.

It was clear that lending countries, international organizations, and debtors all had an interest in fostering interbank cooperation. Lending countries and international organizations wished to ensure that continued credits would be forthcoming from the banks to minimize their burden of bailing out the debtors. The debtors themselves realized it was in their interest to aid large banks in securing funds from smaller banks—even though the unity of banks could prove to be hazardous to their long-term interest in picking off banks one by one.

---

[33]The parish idea is from Fred Hirsch, "The Bagehot Problem," *The Manchester School* 45, 3 (September 1977):241-57.

Jesús Silva Herzog, Mexico's Finance Minister, and Brazilian Central Bank President Carlos Langoni were instrumental in aiding the banks. Silva Herzog suggested a list of about a dozen large banks to serve on an advisory committee.[34] Langoni asked Citibank and Morgan Guaranty to co-chair the general rescue plan for Brazil and then worked closely with them to develop a four-part plan to obtain new loans, reschedule part of Brazil's existing debt, and ensure continued trade credits and interbank deposits. Brazilian officials also presented the plan to Brazil's creditors in December 1982 and then helped in setting up four committees, suggesting who should lead them as well.

As contributions to jumbo loans are not mandatory and are vulnerable to cheating by banks, large banks needed information from debtors to verify compliance. The central bank of Brazil has helped large banks keep track of recalcitrant lenders. Brazil went one step further in helping the rescheduling committee charged with the task of restoring interbank lines. Based on information obtained from the central bank, Banker's Trust was able to send out telexes to all banks indicating who had restored interbank lines and who had not.[35] Furthermore, Langoni sent telexes to different banks telling them where to deposit the loans due from other parts of the rescheduling package.

As part of the effort to encourage recalcitrant banks to participate in jumbo loans, debtors were able to threaten them with a loss of future business when lending returned to "normal."[36] Sometimes, however, threats did not succeed and a more concessionary attitude was necessary. In 1981 the Central Bank of Poland, Bank Handlowy, chose to pay off a floating rate note held by the Banque Nationale de Paris (which was acting as an agent for private investors). This rare action was in response to a threat by investors to declare Poland in default—a tactic also followed by two U.S. banks.[37]

---

[34]Kraft, p. 21.

[35]*Fortune*, 11 July 1983, and interviews with Brazilian officials.

[36]Interviews with bankers.

[37]*Business Week*, 3 May 1982.

Creditor governments used their authoritative positions to encourage cooperation from recalcitrant banks. In December 1982, during the Mexican rescheduling, the Bank of England pressed the British banks to contribute to the Mexican jumbo loan to set an example for the smaller American banks. In telexing its pledge, Lloyd's stated that "We are only doing this because the Bank of England asked us to." [38] Indeed one banker thought that his bank's license would be in danger if they did not cooperate.[39]

While the Bank of England applied the stick, Fed chairman Paul Volcker supplied the carrot, announcing in November 1982 that new credits to countries in need of rescheduling and with agreed-upon IMF programs "should not be subject to supervisory criticism."[40] He helped out again the following May, when he called the top officers of six New York banks into his office and persuaded them to begin a new rescheduling effort.[41]

Not all governments leapt at the chance to bring domestic banks in line. It took a call from De Larosière to his successor at the French Treasury, Michel Camdessus, to spur the latter into action. Camdessus then phoned recalcitrant banks and pressed them to cooperate.[42] Central bank officials in Switzerland, Spain, and Germany were particularly hesitant.[43] Indeed the Fed and the Bank of England had to press more reluctant central banks into action. Intragovernmental disputes hampered these efforts. Though the U.K. Treasury supported the Bank of England's efforts in the Mexican jumbo loan, it later took a tougher stance toward Brazil (where it was unwilling to contribute). As a result, the Bank of England took a lower profile.[44]

---

[38] Quoted in Delamaide, p. 113.

[39] *Euromoney*, January 1983, p. 41.

[40] *Ibid.*, p. 39. The "supervisory criticism" to which Volcker referred was U.S. regulatory policy on limits to sovereign debtors. In many cases, additional loans to debtors would push banks over their loan limits.

[41] *Wall Street Journal*, 30 August 1983.

[42] Interview with French commercial banker.

[43] Interview with Swiss commercial banker.

[44] Interview with British central banker.

Banks were sometimes reluctant to simply accede to government wishes. Commercial banks were often unwilling to extend new credits without being assured by the central banks that other commercial banks were participating as well.

Finally, international organizations were helpful in applying some pressure to resolve the banks' collective action problems. The IMF has more access to information than individual banks, and it can use that information to support the cooperative effort. It prepared a list of 1,400 banks that had made loans to Brazil, matching each with its total exposure. From that information it calculated the amount of each bank's expected contribution.[45]

We have seen that banks faced many obstacles to cooperation — ranging from an inability to bind other banks to agreements to the differences in their capabilities and exposure — which affected their motivation to take united action. Yet banks were successful and have continued to cooperate in the rescheduling efforts in spite of their many differences. The large banks united under American leadership in Latin America and shared many of the costs. Smaller banks were enlisted in the larger banks' efforts. Through the use of various resources, including both carrots and sticks, the large banks ensured that the smaller banks would bear their share of costs. The result was a relatively unified group of banks facing isolated debtors — a sharp improvement from what would have been the case had individual banks alone faced powerful debtors. In this respect, the banks' success has been unmatched by the debtors.

[45]*International Herald Tribune*, 16 December 1982.

4

COOPERATION AMONG DEBTOR COUNTRIES

At first glance, it may seem that debtor countries could benefit from—and would be likely to develop—a united front. The eleven-nation Cartagena group of Latin American debtors owed over $350 billion in early 1985.[1] Although banks as a group may be able to survive the default of any single country,[2] the default of just the four major Latin American debtors together (whose debt equals 83.6 percent of all U.S. bank capital)[3] could bring down the international financial system. This prospect gives the united debtors a leverage over the banks in threatening repudiation that any single debtor does not have.

Debtor governments may also cooperate to avoid a situation where one country secures more favorable treatment from the banks. If a country received less favorable treatment, its officials would be criticized for having negotiated poorly. They would want to make sure they obtained comparable terms and thus had an incentive to cooperate with other debtors in the rescheduling of debts with banks.

Unlike the banks, however, debtor countries have not developed a united negotiating front. The idea of a debtors' cartel was first broached in the fall of 1982. Latin American debtor countries first publicly discussed such a possibility in March 1983 in Panama.[4]

[1] *International Herald Tribune*, 15 February 1983.

[2] A Brazilian default could spell the collapse of Citicorp and Manufacturers Hanover, exposed to the tune of 71.2 and 66.1 percent of capital respectively (Batista, p. 20).

[3] Dale and Mattione, p. 14.

[4] Note that non-Latin debtors have not even broached the topic of a debtors' cartel.

Subsequent talks in Caracas in September 1983, Quito in January 1984, Cartagena in June 1984, and Mar del Plata in September 1984 have failed to produce effective collective action. Situational factors worked strongly against coordinated action among Latin American debtors, and even the most strenuous efforts of some of the smaller debtors to form a cartel were doomed to failure.

OBSTACLES TO A DEBTORS' CARTEL

As in other cases of attempted cartels, if the debtors begin to act collectively, they face the possibility that one of their number may succumb to incentives offered by banks, creditor governments, or international organizations and break ranks. Since the debtors are sovereign countries interacting in an anarchic situation, there is no higher body to whom they can appeal in order to enforce cooperation from recalcitrants.

The functional similarity of debtor countries, moreover, places them in an adversarial relationship as they compete for funds. All debtors are similar in that they would like to attract funds from creditors for development purposes. In general, the larger debtors recognize that they have been more successful in securing loans than smaller, poorer debtors. Indeed Mexico, Argentina, and Brazil managed to obtain 52.1 percent of all U.S. bank claims on non-OPEC developing countries before September 1982.[5]

Debtors face different internal political constraints which bear on their efforts to implement adjustment plans. Mexico in 1983 rapidly instituted various measures that at least temporarily improved its financial position—at high political cost for its leadership. When President Raúl Alfonsin in Argentina had a hard time in getting trade unions to agree to slower wage growth in 1984 and as a result called for debtor unity and concessions from banks, one Mexican official remarked as follows:

> We agree with Alfonsin's warning that the crisis is not over, but the fact is that we immediately took internal measures to stabilize our economy and he did not. It's only reasonable for banks to consider us a lesser risk than Argentina.[6]

[5] June 1982 figures from Dale and Mattione, p. 14.

[6] *New York Times*, 23 September 1984.

Alfonsin's hard line in negotiating with the IMF worried the Mexicans. One official in the Mexican Foreign Ministry complained, "We have a lot of incentives to convince the other nations to be cautious. We have suffered a lot to get where we are, and we don't want to see them upset it."[7]

The most significant factor hindering cooperation among debtors is the wide variation in their size and total debt burdens. As of late 1984 the Latin American countries involved in rescheduling arrangements owed banks sums ranging from $661 million in Guyana to $102 billion in Brazil.[8] These countries differ tremendously in terms of GNP, per capita income, degree of industrialization, and trade patterns.

Of course asymmetrical distributions of capabilities can be conducive to the development of stable arrangements—if the largest or larger powers expect to gain from a cartel arrangement. In Latin America, however, the major countries were less than enthusiastic about such an idea. Because of their large markets and shares of bank capital, Mexico, Brazil, and Venezuela were able to negotiate better terms than Uruguay or Bolivia. Furthermore, Mexico, one of the first countries to experience a severe financial crisis, was in a unique position. Since it has a lengthy border with the United States, the U.S. government was clearly interested in ensuring that Mexico obtain a settlement with banks that would not lead to political instability and greater Mexican emigration to the United States. Mexican officials were aware of their special position and saw little gain from aligning with debtors having less leverage.

In sum, the situational factors have not proved conducive to the formation of a debtors' cartel. Some efforts in this direction have been made, yet none have succeeded.

BARGAINING AMONG DEBTORS

As could be expected, it was the small countries, with the least individual bargaining leverage, who made the first calls for a

[7] *Wall Street Journal*, 2 April 1984.

[8] The Guyana figure dates from the end of 1983 (Institute of International Finance).

debtors' cartel. Such countries have a more difficult time in securing new funds as part of their rescheduling packages. They do not pose a systemic risk and therefore do not garner support from either creditor countries or international organizations. According to one investment banker,

> The IMF, which in the cases of Mexico, Brazil, and a couple other countries such as Yugoslavia, played a crucial role in "arm-twisting" commercial banks and "forcing" them to lend billions of dollars in additional money, has exerted little efforts [sic] in assisting smaller debtors in mobilizing additional external financing.[9]

Even though these smaller countries were highly motivated to seek cooperation, they had few power resources to draw upon. There is little precedent for cooperation among Latin American countries. Andean Pact efforts to develop a common negotiating front on foreign direct investment soon met with failure as participants fell into competition with each other. Similarly, Latin American Common Market discussions have not led to sustained cooperation.[10] With the two largest debtors, Mexico and Brazil, opposing the formation of a cartel, there was no actor to play the role of a hegemon (as Saudi Arabia has done in OPEC). Smaller countries had little to offer by way of side payments to encourage cooperation. Having few overall resources, they could not use linkages to other issue areas to their advantage.

Time also works against the debtors. If they are going to be interacting on this issue after the "debt-bomb" has been defused (or exploded), it will be as adversaries as they compete for funds once again. Indeed after the Latin American countries defaulted in mass in the late 1820s (they were not, however, allied with each

---

[9]Statement of Christine Bindert in Joint Economic Committee of the U.S. Senate and House, Subcommittee on Economic Goals and Intergovernmental Policy, *Dealing with the Debt Problem of Latin America*, 98th Congress, 2d session, 13 November 1984, p. 38.

[10]For a discussion, see Roger Fontaine, *The Andean Pact: A Political Analysis* (Beverly Hills, Calif.: Sage Publications, 1977); Washington Papers 5, 45.

other), they found themselves competing for funds three decades later.[11]

Not only are smaller countries without power among other debtors, but banks, creditor governments, and international organizations in the 1980s were all actively working against their efforts to develop a united front. Indeed as one advisor to the Latin American Economic System in Caracas pointed out, the banks and the U.S. government "are dissuading the Latin nations from collaborating by promising more rapid treatment if they act alone."[12]

The only successful attempts at coordination among debtors so far have promoted cooperation, and not confrontation, with the banks. Mexico lent $50 million to Costa Rica in March 1984. At the same time, it engineered an agreement to help the Argentines make interest payments before a 31 March deadline — thereby saving the banks from having to put the Argentine loans into nonperforming status (see below). This effort was designed to show good faith by the debtors in the hope of getting the banks to offer them better terms in the future. The Colombian Finance Minister claimed that Argentina now had a "moral commitment" to its new lenders, who advised it to "play by the rules."[13]

In sum, debtors have been unable to unite to press for major concessions from banks because the larger debtor countries have felt they would be more successful on their own and smaller debtors have lacked the resources to overcome large-debtor resistance. Individual debtors were left facing a unified coalition of banks, leaving a serious potential for stalemated negotiations.

[11]See Jenks.

[12]*Institutional Investor*, July 1984, p. 233.

[13]*Wall Street Journal*, 18 June 1984.

5

FORCING A SETTLEMENT: THE ROLE OF CREDITOR GOVERNMENTS AND INTERNATIONAL ORGANIZATIONS

With banks unwilling to budge on concessionary terms in the rescheduling, and debtors resisting bank arguments that the consequences of repudiation would prove worse than yielding to bank demands, the prospects were grim for a successful resolution of the 1982-84 debt crisis. However, creditor countries and international organizations feared a breakdown in the international financial system, leading them to break the stalemate between debtors and banks. It is to this broader picture that we now turn.

In the first part of this chapter, we will examine why creditor governments and international organizations were motivated to participate in the debt negotiations with banks and were willing to share some of the costs of reschedulings. We will see how banks and other lenders were able to overcome their initial differences to attain cooperation, and how they used various strategies to shift costs to other parties.

The second part of this chapter will focus on the debtors' efforts to link outside issues to debt rescheduling in an attempt to enlist the aid of the creditor governments on their behalf. We will see how creditor governments have to some degree restrained banks from pushing sovereign debtors to the brink of economic collapse.

BARGAINING AMONG BANKS, CREDITOR GOVERNMENTS, AND INTERNATIONAL ORGANIZATIONS

INCENTIVES

The banks sought the aid of international organizations and creditor governments both to put greater pressure on debtors to agree to terms and to solicit contributions of new financing and information.[1] But even without bank prodding these actors were motivated to participate actively in the rescheduling.

The drastic reduction of imports by the heavily indebted countries in response to the crisis had deleterious consequences for manufacturing interests in northern markets. U.S. Under Secretary of Commerce Lionel Olmer estimated that a sharp drop in Mexican imports alone from 1981 to 1982 may have resulted in the loss of as many as a quarter of a million jobs for U.S. workers.[2] Federal Reserve Chairman Volcker stressed this point to a Senate subcommittee investigating international debt:

> In all of this, the mutual dependency of the U.S. economy and the stability of the international financial system should be apparent. Failure to deal successfully with the immediate international pressures could only jeopardize prospects for *our* recovery—for *our* jobs, for *our* export markets, and for *our* financial markets (emphasis in original).[3]

Creditor governments realize that only they can help in providing immediate short-term aid in a crisis situation. On 12 August 1982, Mexican Foreign Minister Silva Herzog notified U.S. Treasury Secretary Donald Regan, Paul Volcker, and Jacques De Larosière that his country was unable to continue servicing its debt. ($10 billion was due in the next few months.) The next day he flew to Washington, and during what is now called the "Mexican Weekend," various U.S. government agencies were able to extend $1 billion in credit

[1]We have already seen in Chapter 3 how the large banks sought the aid of these actors in building interbank cooperation.

[2]Statement of Lionel Olmer in U.S. Senate, Committee on Banking, Housing, and Urban Affairs, Subcommittee on International Finance and Monetary Policy, *Export-Import Bank Proposal of Credit to Brazil and Mexico*, 98th Congress, 1st session, 14 September 1983, p. 17. A Treasury official estimated 250,000 lost jobs as a result of a drop in exports to all Latin America from 1981 to 1983; statement of George Hoguet, Principal Assistant Secretary of the Treasury for International Affairs, before the Council of the Americas, 8 December 1984, *U.S. Treasury Notes.*

[3]U.S. Senate, Committee on Banking, Housing, and Urban Affairs, Subcommittee on International Finance and Monetary Policy, *International Debt*, 98th Congress, 1st session, 14, 15, and 17 February 1983, p. 288.

guarantees, another $1 billion up front for oil purchases (at lower than market rates), and $300 million from the Fed. Furthermore, Volcker helped get the European central banks to join in putting together a $1.5 billion loan from the Bank for International Settlements (BIS)—of which the United States contributed half.

Central banks in particular can act as lenders of last resort during a financial emergency because of their relatively autonomous position in domestic politics. In the late 1920s it was they who were called upon to stem a series of crises in Europe, brought about by sovereign debtor defaults and central bank runs. Yet these efforts could not be sustained, culminating in a wave of defaults from 1931 to 1933.[4]

Charged with ensuring the stability of the international financial system, international organizations would like to cooperate with banks to stave off a crisis.[5] Like governments, international organizations are capable of rapidly mobilizing large amounts of emergency finance (witness the spate of IMF and BIS loans). But even though the banks are capable of supplying larger amounts of funds than international organizations in the long run, they are unable to impose adjustment programs on debtor governments. The banks lack these organizations' capacity to monitor the economic performance of sovereign governments. In spite of often adversarial relations, debtor countries are usually more willing to submit to IMF scrutiny (they are, after all, members of that organization) than they are to give some 1,400 commercial banks access to privileged information. When the banks tried to negotiate an adjustment package without IMF participation in Peru in the 1970s, the Peruvians refused to comply.

OBSTACLES

Creditor governments, banks, and international organizations have different objectives behind their mutual interest to cooperate. Governments often have foreign policy objectives that have little

---

[4]For more on this period, see in particular Clarke, Kindleberger, and Fishlow.

[5]The most important international organizations in short-term crisis management have been the IMF and the BIS. Hence the following discussion concentrates on their role.

salience for bankers. As one Treasury official noted, "Our interest in an orderly resolution of these problems stems not only from our economic interests ... but our political and strategic interests."[6] Upon announcing the March 1984 Argentina rescue plan, Secretary Regan justified U.S. participation under these same lines:

> We recognize that here was a new government, less than a hundred days in office when this crisis started to develop . . . freely elected, beset by the left and right—we wanted to try and help that government because we believe in democracy and believe in trying to help Latin American countries that have freely elected governments.[7]

Such political concerns have been of little import to bankers. Quipped one Citicorp vice chairman, "Who knows which political system works? The only test we care about is: Can they pay their bills?"[8]

The banks and the IMF have conflicts of interest that have arisen out of their different functions. They would like to ensure continued debt service, but they recognize that this requires an additional influx of capital. Banks may be much more interested in earning immediate profits than are international organizations concerned with global financial stability, and may be unwilling to make any concessionary loans to buy time. International organizations, on the other hand, may be interested in curing the disease, not just alleviating the symptoms.

The internal characteristics of the different participants pose some important constraints on cooperative behavior. Governments in particular must to varying degrees respond to the vagaries of domestic politics. The Reagan administration faced a populist Congressional opposition in passing its increased 1983 contribution to the IMF and in clearing proposed increased Export-Import Bank guarantees to Brazil and Mexico.[9] Indeed a Treasury official felt

---

[6]Statement of George Hoguet before the Council of the Americas.

[7]Press conference, Washington, D.C., 31 March 1984.

[8]*Wall Street Journal*, 21 December 1981.

[9]One Republican Congressional staffer in an interview commented that although his boss supported the IMF bill in principle, he would receive too

compelled to make the following disclaimer with respect to the aforementioned Argentine rescue:

> This was not a "bank bailout" by American taxpayers. ... We were motivated by our desire to support the new democratic government in Argentina ... not just to help U.S. banks avoid reporting earnings losses for the first quarter of 1984.[10]

The IMF is also constrained by its internal structure as it depends on contributions from member countries to maintain its capital base. It has recently been running short of funds, and there is talk of allowing it to borrow additional funds on the open market.

Successful cooperation among these actors can be imperiled by another key obstacle: each would like the others to bear a greater share of the cost of stabilizing the international credit market. This hurdle to policy coordination was raised by each actor's fear that any additional funds it contributed would merely be used to pay off others. Again the situation is analogous to a game of chicken (although, as we shall see, there is a degree of hierarchy involved here).

The Treasury has time and again stressed that any funds it contributes to rescheduling packages are simply bailouts for the banks. In the words of one Treasury official, "Our approach stresses official finance as a catalyst rather than as a substitute for private finance. ... It is imperative that commercial banks and non-official creditors share in the burden."[11] In the debate over Export-Import Bank guarantees for Brazil and Mexico, Marc Leland, U.S. Assistant Secretary of the Treasury for International Affairs, told a Senate sub-committee that

---

much constituent flak from his conservative district for "bailing out the banks" and hence voted against it. For a discussion of the domestic politics surrounding this issue, see Vinod K. Aggarwal and Ronald Gutfleish, "U.S., Help the IMF," *New York Times*, 27 September 1983.

[10]Statement of David Mulford, Assistant Secretary for International Affairs, before the U.S. House of Representatives, Committee on Banking, Finance, and Urban Affairs, Subcommittee on International Trade, Investment, and Monetary Policy, 1 May 1984.

[11]Statement of George Hoguet before the Council of the Americas.

the facilities could be specifically linked to continued commercial financing. The distribution of the financing burden between private and official creditors must be equitable. It is essential that commercial banks continue to contribute their share of new financing and risk-taking.[12]

In their relations with each other, commercial banks and the IMF face the same problem of an equitable allocation of the burden. Even if they had the same objectives, they could still run into systemic obstacles to cooperation. Although they might agree to cooperate in extending joint loans, neither party can be absolutely sure that the other will make additional contributions that may be necessary for debtors to maintain loan servicing in the future. Both the IMF and central banks worry that one lender will be paid back at the other's expense.

The problems of achieving cooperation between banks and international organizations are illustrated by a 1979 Turkish crisis. Under OECD and IMF sponsorship, a $5.1 billion rescheduling arrangement was developed to which the banks contributed no new money. Yet a good deal of this money went right into the hands of the banks—leading one IMF man to complain that "We constantly told the banks that they were taking out the money that the IMF and governments were putting in. But they wanted their interest."[13] In like manner, a 1981 IMF agreement with Romania was derailed when banks curtailed credit flows.[14]

This problem of burden allocation was explicitly recognized in negotiations within the U.S. government over the 1983 bill for IMF contributions. The Treasury agreed to an amendment to the bill which required the American executive director of the IMF to oppose any IMF loans "for the purpose of repaying loans which have been imprudently made by banking institutions."[15]

---

[12]In *Export-Import Bank Proposal of Credit to Brazil and Mexico*.

[13]*Euromoney*, January 1983, p. 38.

[14]*Ibid.*

[15]Robert N. McCauley, "IMF: Managed Lending"; in *World Debt Crisis: International Lending on Trial*, ed. Michael P. Claudon (Cambridge: Ballinger, 1986).

The banks are afraid of losing IMF participation. As one U.S. banker noted, "We can't really have a situation preserved where we come in at the IMF's behest and then find that they get out before the commercial banks can, otherwise we'd lose the element of conditionality."[16] Even when the IMF has not been directly involved in debt rescheduling negotiations—as in 1986 discussions of Brazil's debt to commercial banks—the banks have been wary of offending the IMF. Brazil refused to submit to an IMF adjustment plan, normally part of the negotiations with commercial bankers. Still, "The country's foreign bankers did not want to be seen to snub the IMF," and hence de Larosière of the IMF gave his tacit approval to Brazil's economic policies.[17]

The problem of enforcing binding commitments is not as severe for banks and creditor governments—linked in a subordinate-superordinate relationship—as it is for anarchic bank-international organization interaction.[18] Because of the hierarchy in the former case, the creditor governments can legitimately impose their will on the banks. In particular, they can use regulatory means. The Securities and Exchange Commission's announcement in November 1982 that banks would have to report exposure totaling more than one percent of capital was resented by the banks, who were afraid of making confidential information public.[19] One senior U.S. Treasury official nicely summed up the relationship between the banks and the Fed as follows: "Whatever their legal rights, banks don't want to annoy the Federal Reserve. It pays to maintain good relations with the Fed."[20] But while governments might simply impose their will in negotiations, they have reasons to avoid doing so. For example, they fear that their foreign policy goals or domestic support could be undermined. Indeed U.S. Treasury Secretary

---

[16]*Euromoney*, January 1983, p. 44.

[17]*The Economist*, 8 March 1986, p. 83.

[18]Note that creditor countries have allied among themselves through the Cook Committee of the BIS in an effort to maintain their regulatory capabilities vis-à-vis the banks (see Richard Dale, *Bank Supervision Around the World* [New York: Group of Thirty, 1983]).

[19]*The Banker*, January 1983, p. 22.

[20]Interview with senior U.S. Treasury official.

James Baker argued the following before a joint IMF-World Bank committee:

> [Commercial bank lending] is an element over which industrial country governments can have only limited influence. . . . Our governments must avoid specific intervention in the commercial decision-making process of our private institutions."[21]

In sum, both banks and governments recognize their mutual political dependence. Neither would like to antagonize the other since the costs of conflict can be high.

NEGOTIATIONS

Because governments are reluctant to impose their will on the banks and the IMF is unable to do so, bargaining must be used to resolve conflicts among these organizations. Governments have means other than their superordinate position with which to influence bank behavior, and vice versa. Each is privy to different sources of information. Information-sharing is a particularly sensitive issue for banks. They would prefer not to share confidential information with governments, fearing that competitors might obtain it. With respect to material resources, we have noted that although governments can provide a large amount of money quickly, it is the banks who have access to the largest amount of capital. (In none of the major rescheduling efforts did official contributions exceed those from the private sphere.) Indeed Assistant Secretary of the Treasury McNamar stressed the point that the U.S. government's role in the 1982 Mexican package was only to provide short-term liquidity.[22] In addition, banks and governments interact over a range of issues, and over a long period of time as well. Governments require access to commercial credit for industrial policy,[23] and the banks are continually seeking government assistance on regulatory issues.

---

[21]Statement before the meetings of the Interim Committee of the IMF and the Development Committee of the World Bank and IMF.

[22]Press conference, Washington, D.C., 20 August 1982.

[23]While on the whole the United States refrains from engaging in industrial policy, the Chrysler bailout—where the government needed the cooperation of the commercial banks—is one case in which it did.

Although not involved in a hierarchical relation, the IMF can exert some control over the banks. It has much better information about the economic health of debtors than do the banks. (Recall that it was the IMF who calculated the contributions from participant banks in the Brazilian jumbo loan.) It constantly monitors their economic performance, yet is not always willing (or allowed) to share this information with them. In general, though, the IMF works through member country central banks to exert influence on commercial banks.

International organizations, particularly the IMF, were instrumental in inducing rescue efforts by the central and commercial banks during the 1982-84 crisis. In November 1982 the IMF made an unprecedented demand that commercial banks commit themselves to raising $5 billion and official creditors $2 billion in additional lending to Mexico before it would approve that country's adjustment package and contribute new funds of its own. Before that time, the banks had made an IMF agreement a prerequisite for continued bank lending. With such large sums at stake, the IMF was unwilling to go ahead with an adjustment program for which the major portion of necessary funds had not yet been committed. As a result, the other creditors were given an additional push to cooperate—at least if they wanted a more effective monitoring of debtor performance.

Banks and creditor governments (particularly the United States) have cooperated to some degree in extending new credits. In addition to regulatory consideration, the U.S. Treasury apparently guaranteed a $600 million bridge loan to Brazil from six commercial banks in November 1982.[24] Furthermore, the Treasury increased the amount of its own $1.23 billion November 1982 bridge loan (to $1.93 billion the following February) because of Brazil's difficulties in maintaining its interbank credit lines. The Treasury also played a role in helping both the banks' balance sheets and Argentina by guaranteeing a $400 million short-term loan on 30 March 1984 from eleven commercial banks and the central banks of Mexico, Brazil, Colombia, and Venezuela. If Argentina had not paid overdue

[24]Delamaide, p. 119.

interest by the end of the following day, the U.S. banks would have had to classify its loans as nonperforming.[25]

The most recent significant proposal for the management of the debt crisis put forth by creditor governments is the so-called Baker Plan. In a speech to the joint annual meeting of the World Bank and IMF in 1985, James Baker proposed a three-part program to deal with the debt crisis. First, he asked commercial banks to provide $20 billion in additional loans to the fifteen largest problem debtors over the next three years. Second, he called on the World Bank and the Inter-American Development Bank to furnish an extra $9 billion to these same debtors over the next three years. Third, he suggested that the $2.7 billion expected in repayments over the next six years from countries who had borrowed from the IMF be targeted to help resolve the balance of payments problems of the poorest (mainly African) debtors.[26] In return, debtors would follow "market oriented" policies to streamline their economies. The measures envisaged by Baker include mobilizing domestic savings, encouraging domestic and foreign investment, liberalizing trade, and reducing export subsidies.[27]

Although supported as a step forward by most bankers and debtors, the Baker Plan does not significantly deviate from the case-by-case approach to adjustment that has been the norm. Moreover, the loans that will be provided do not go very far toward meeting the need for large capital inflows. According to one observer, while the banks might be resistant to providing additional loans given their highly exposed positions, the money is "peanuts" from their perspective.[28] As noted below, the grave problems encountered by Mexico as a result of the sharp fall in oil prices challenge the adequacy of the Baker Plan.

---

[25]Not all creditor governments and banks were pleased with the Argentine operation. One British central banker commented in an interview that "The U.S. didn't do a brilliant job," arguing that this deal undermined Argentina's incentive to reach an agreement with the IMF.

[26]*The Economist,* 12 October 1985, pp. 75-76.

[27]*New York Times,* 9 October 1985.

[28]*The Economist,* 19 October 1985, p. 90.

DEBTORS' LINKAGE STRATEGY

Just as banks capitalized on the desire of creditor governments and international organizations to reach an agreement on debt rescheduling by shifting some of the costs to these actors, so too did debtors. As we have noted, creditor governments' foreign policy concerns often outweigh their interests in having their banks emerge unscathed from debt rescheduling. Continued lending may add to a creditor government's influence in foreign affairs. For instance, Chancellor Helmut Schmidt was disappointed about the small size of a West German consortium's loan to Poland in August 1980 because he wanted to give Polish leader Edward Gierek a "warm welcome" at an upcoming meeting in Hemburg.[29] As discussed above, in December 1983 the Reagan administration pushed the U.S. banks to be flexible in negotiating with the Argentines "as a gesture of goodwill toward the new democratic authorities."[30] This tactic enraged the banks. In the words of one banker, "We expected to get facts and figures, a detailed picture of the country's medium- to long-term economic plans. All we got were platitudes about Argentina's new democracy."[31]

As country-risk analysts have long recognized, the domestic politics in a debtor country often place overwhelming obstacles in the path to adjustment and continued debt-servicing. Austerity programs necessarily impose substantial economic costs. Debtors have thus pointed to their governments' fragile domestic positions when appealing to creditor governments for help in their negotiations with the banks and the IMF. Just as one can improve his chances in a game of chicken by showing that his hands are tied, the debtors have tried to show that their hands are tied as well.[32] Argentina, Brazil, and Peru (among others) have all played this card, com-

---

[29] *The Economist*, 16 August 1980, p. 58.

[30] *Financial Times*, 15 December 1983.

[31] *Financial Times*, 1 February 1984.

[32] Throwing out the steering wheel or jumping in the back seat in a game between cars are effective strategies in a game of chicken. Argentina's negotiations over debt rescheduling resemble such a strategy.

plaining that they cannot bear any more of the adjustment burden without abandoning their fragile democratic regimes.

There is no doubt that adjustment has had a traumatic effect on their economies. In 1983 Under Secretary of Commerce Olmer told the subcommittee holding hearings on the Export-Import Bank that 76 percent of Mexican private businesses were anticipating losses and 15 percent were already in liquidation.[33] More recently it has been estimated that since mid-1982 the real wages of the Mexican working class have fallen to levels of twenty-three years ago.[34] Politically this has resulted in huge demonstrations for a debt moratorium. Similar problems have beset other debtors. One analyst has noted that the buying power of the Brazilian middle class was expected to fall 30 percent in 1984 alone.[35]

Debtor governments have complained about recent increases in trade protection in an attempt to make creditor governments see their side of their struggle with the banks. The Foreign Minister of Argentina, Dante Caputo, remarked as follows:

> What we are seeking from the industrial countries is the acceptance of the need to place the debt discussions in the framework of a political dialogue. The issues involved can't be limited to negotiations with bankers.[36]

This linkage has been resisted for the most part (at least in public) by creditors. According to the *Los Angeles Times*,

> The refusal of the Reagan Administration to give the Latin American debt "political status" has been a principal obstacle to a broadening of the debt negotiations to include governments, which control trade politics, interest rates by central banks, and contributions of capital to institutions.[37]

---

[33] *Export-Import Bank Proposal of Credit to Brazil and Mexico*, p. 17.

[34] *New York Times*, 10 February 1986.

[35] Riordan Roett in *Adjustment Crisis in the Third World*, ed. Richard Feinberg and Valeriana Kallab (New Brunswick: Transaction Books, 1985), p. 150.

[36] *International Herald Tribune*, 15 February 1985.

[37] Quoted in *International Herald Tribune*, 15 February 1985.

Yet behind the scenes, the story has been somewhat different. The Treasury, State Department, and other agencies in the U.S. government "have been seeking ways to ease them [debtors] through the balance-of-payments difficulties that have been made worse by the world recession and high interest rates."[38]

The debtors have succeeded to some degree in their efforts. In its December 1983 agreement, Mexico managed to gain a one percent reduction in the interest rate it had been paying on bailout financing after Fed Chairman Volcker "in a rare intervention" sided with it during negotiations for new terms. The bankers on Mexico's advisory committee were told that Volcker "encouraged the Mexican proposal," an announcement that came as a surprise to the bankers. The director of Mexico's Department of Public Credit, Angel Gurria, noted that this issue had been discussed at the "highest levels" of the U.S. and Mexican governments. Indeed one U.S. official remarked that this was the "first time I can recall [that] a U.S. bank regulator—who is not supposed to be involved in matters of foreign policy—is taking sides with the debtor and pressing U.S. banks into concessions."[39]

A "tied-hands" approach worked for Brazil in the fall of 1983. The Brazilian Congress rejected an IMF agreement to keep public-sector salary raises to 80 percent of the cost of living increase, and yet President João Figuereido succeeded in getting creditor government support for less stringent measures. According to the *Financial Times*, "With the endorsement of their central banks, commercial banks have accepted the principle that they too must make some sacrifices in terms of cash flow and profit to aid the stricken borrowers."[40] In this vein, Volcker promised U.S. banks that in the Brazilian case the Fed would not enforce regulations requiring them to reclassify loans that had been rescheduled on more lenient terms, and the Bank of England "spoke forcibly" in favor of the loans as well.[41]

[38] *New York Times*, 28 March 1984.

[39] *Wall Street Journal*, 4 January 1984.

[40] 10 October 1983.

[41] *Financial Times*, 13 and 19 October 1983.

Argentina was also successful in enlisting U.S. aid (as noted above). When, after its return to an elected government in December 1984, it remained firm in its negotiations with the IMF, the U.S. Treasury, as well as several central and commercial banks, came to its aid with the March 1984 bailout package. In effect, this action undermined the position of IMF negotiators. Afterwards an Argentine official at a U.S. bank subsidiary noted the following:

> From the Argentine standpoint, they have obtained what they were looking for. . . . From now on, it won't be Argentina dealing alone with the banks and the International Monetary Fund. The U.S. government will be there too.[42]

Creditor governments are worried about the future as well. Deputy Secretary of the Treasury McNamar, after noting that debtors are having problems with their adjustment plans, told an audience in January 1984 that "creditor banks must set aside additional reserves against losses."[43] We have noted that U.S. banks oppose rescheduling debts over longer terms and lower rates because they would have to write them off as nonperforming if interest payments were delayed or reduced. If U.S. officials, like their European counterparts, succeed in these efforts to encourage extra provisioning, then this major obstacle will be overcome.

[42] *Wall Street Journal*, 13 April 1984.

[43] Remarks before the Davos Symposium, Davos, Switzerland, 30 January 1984.

6

CONCLUSION AND PROSPECTS

AGREEMENTS AND DISTRIBUTION OF COSTS AMONG ACTORS

We have analyzed the international politics of debt rescheduling. Starting from what appeared to be an almost impossible situation for securing agreement, with banks facing debtors who appeared to have the upper hand, banks achieved agreements favorable to them. They did so by allying with creditor governments and international organizations and played upon the concerns of the latter two actors about the stability of the financial system. By contrast, debtors failed to develop a unified stance, although they too secured some help from creditor governments and international organizations. The distribution of costs and benefits among banks and debtors is clearly not symmetrical. As we shall see, there is a close correspondence between political and economic success. We turn first to the approach that has developed in resolving the immediate debt problem and then to the distribution of costs among the actors.

It is beginning to look as if a distinctive pattern is developing for debt rescheduling. According to Laurence Brainard, a senior vice-president of Bankers Trust, "An understanding has developed among the banks on the methods of approaching reschedulings. Nowhere is it codified, but there are understood priorities."[1] We have witnessed the following pattern: (1) debtors unable to stay current on their payments seek an IMF loan and a rescheduling accord with commercial banks; (2) they work out an adjustment plan with the IMF, under which the commercial banks will be required to advance funds as well; (3) the official debt is negotiated through the Paris Club (the name given to the meetings between official creditor

[1]*Euromoney*, July 1983, p. 55.

governments and debtors); (4) the banks contribute additional funds in accordance with IMF directives; (5) the BIS or individual creditor countries may make a loan to tide over a debtor until the money from the banks and the IMF comes through; and (6) the IMF monitors a debtor's progress on the adjustment plan.

There have of course been deviations from this pattern. In the original Mexican rescheduling, Mexico sought immediate aid from the United States to tide it over until it had settled with the IMF. In the case of Venezuela, there has been no IMF loan, but this organization is still involved in monitoring the accord that Venezuela reached with the banks.

In general, the banks have been forced to pay some costs in the form of losses on some portion of their assets, but by and large they have escaped relatively unscathed. Although bank shares have shown sharp declines, banks have been able to preserve their capital and avoid huge losses. Moreover, they have not contributed significant additional funds as part of the long-term reschedulings, nor have they reduced interest rates below the market rate.

In contrast, debtors are undergoing painful adjustments with high economic and political costs. Growth rates are often negative, and unemployment has risen sharply. Business failures have reached unprecedented levels. Moreover, after the crisis debtors have found themselves in the position of major capital exporters. One study estimates that there was a negative capital outflow (profit remittances and interest) of $30 billion from the major debtors in 1982 and 1983 alone.[2]

Creditor countries have recouped most of the funds contributed to debtors and currently have agreements on long-term repayments through the Paris Club. In the strategic realm, the United States, for example, has not suffered any major setbacks from the crisis that could benefit Soviet interests—at least in the short run. Debtors recognize that they cannot turn to the East for new financial flows and have instead been forced to intensify their dependence on Western governments.

The IMF and BIS have also not faced any financial losses. By following a strategy of releasing loans in tranches to the debtors

[2]ECLAC, *External Debt in Latin America* (Boulder, Colo.: Lynne Reiner, 1985), pp. 12-13.

instead of in a lump sum, the IMF has retained control over the adjustment process. It frequently has held back scheduled disbursements until it was satisfied that debtors were complying with its programs.

The most significant development in the debt crisis (aside from the Baker Plan) after the initial "fire-fighting" actions has been the Mexican multiyear rescheduling arrangement negotiated in the fall of 1984 and signed in 1985. It appeared at the time that this agreement would be the model for debt rescheduling; it was followed by similar agreements between banks and Venezuela, and discussions along similar lines with other debtors were in the works. The Mexican agreement was strongly supported by creditor countries and involved close cooperation among the banks, Mexico, and the IMF.

The agreement postponed principal payments of $20.1 billion due between 1985 and 1990 and $23.6 billion in previous restructuring pacts into a fourteen-year loan. Aside from the innovation of extending the maturity of the loan, two important changes in the loan were significant. First, the loan allowed non-U.S. banks to switch up to 40 percent of their loan into home currencies. This clause potentially helped European banks, who had faced a strengthening dollar which forced them to increase their reserves to meet domestic regulatory guidelines. Second, the agreement called for continued monitoring of Mexico's performance by the IMF even after its adjustment program expires at the end of 1986. The IMF will give the banks its annual and mid-year consultation reports. Banks having 33 percent of the commitments of the original $5 billion jumbo loan can initiate a vote on the viability of Mexico's position based on the IMF's reports. In addition, to increase their leverage, the banks have asked Mexico to seek official assistance if it needs further capital and is unable to raise it through normal market channels.

OUTLOOK FOR THE FUTURE

We expect the pattern discussed above to continue for the foreseeable future—for political reasons. We have seen how various factors have operated to push the banks, creditor governments,

international organizations, and debtor countries toward cooperation. We have also seen how actors have used various resources to
overcome obstacles. We do not expect this cooperation to break
down, although conflict over the sharing of costs will intensify
among the participants.

At present, the crisis is manageable, but two potential conflicts
could send it out of control. On the one hand, increasingly dis-
enchanted U.S. regional and European banks may break ranks
with the American money-center banks. Regional banks and the
Europeans are not on the whole heavily exposed at this point and
have increasingly made provisions for questionable debt. On the
other hand, debtor countries may find themselves unable to comply
with IMF-prescribed adjustment packages. They may find the domestic costs of continued compliance too overwhelming.

These are serious problems, yet they can be overcome. The
regional banks cannot afford the consequences of leaving the money-
center banks to cope on their own. They require continued interaction
with them. Still, the large American banks may have to start making
some concessions, particularly toward the Europeans. They cannot
simply treat them as satellites. American banks may have to follow
the European example and increase their provisions against questionable debt, and they may also have to start considering interest
capitalization—that is, the automatic conversion of interest due into
additional principal. A change in U.S. regulatory policy would
encourage and facilitate both of these moves.

The debtors are not likely to repudiate their obligations, but
can be pushed only so far with the prescribed adjustment and repayment programs. Debtors are more frequently talking about linking
debt servicing to export receipts and are showing greater reluctance
to follow IMF programs. The banks recognize this fact yet continue
to push the debtors *almost* to the breaking point. The IMF prescrip-
tions remain strict, in part to garner the support of the bankers.

The debtors' breaking point may change. The nature of the
fragile consensus that has been forged among actors is illustrated by
Mexico's recent problems. In spite of the multiyear rescheduling
effort, the Mexican government faced a deep cut in its revenues
with the abrupt fall in oil prices in the second half of 1985 and early
1986. In February 1986 President Miguel de la Madrid announced

that his country intended to limit repayments according to Mexico's ability to pay.[3]

Fear of Mexican debt repudiation abated at the end of June 1986, when Mexico made interest payments on its $98 billion debt. In July 1986 Mexico signed an agreement with the IMF which provisionally linked commodity export prices (oil) and/or slow domestic growth, on the one hand, and automatic extension of new loans, on the other. From July to August Mexican rhetoric grew bolder in negotiations with the banks. In addition to pursuing a similar commodity/loan link, its negotiators demanded interest rate concessions and extremely long maturities on rescheduled debt. Banks resisted these proposals. The danger from their perspective was that such actions could set a precedent for other debtors, such as Argentina, Brazil, and Chile, who might try to link debt to other commodity prices.

Agreement was reached in the week before the September 1986 World Bank-IMF annual meeting on a $12 billion package of new loans for Mexico, half to be provided by commercial banks and half by multinational and official sources. Nearly half ($43.7 billion) of previously rescheduled debt was rescheduled again. Spreads were reduced to less than one percentage point over the London Inter-Bank Offer Rate (LIBOR), and the rescheduled past debt was given an unprecedented twenty-year maturity. Still the agreement was widely perceived to be a failure in Mexico and throughout Latin America since Mexico had sought much more. Banks ultimately refused to accept compensatory financing or lowered interest rates linked directly to a floor on international oil prices, substituting the weaker clause that new loans would be available on a "flexible" basis. Banks also bargained with creditor governments and received guarantees from multinational organizations for a portion of the new bank loans—in essence an explicit (if indirect) promise by industrial country governments that banks would be repaid.[4] In the wake of Mexico's comparative failure to achieve its objectives, explicit cooperation with Argentina and Brazil has begun to look more

[3] *Wall Street Journal*, 24 February 1986.

[4] See *The Banker*, July 1986, and *Latin American Weekly Report* for 7 August and 16 October 1986 for additional details.

attractive. Recently these two countries have intensified their trade and other economic links and are making significant overtures to Mexico.

Other debtors have also announced that their breaking point has been reached. Since President García took office in July 1985, Peru has taken the most radical renegotiation stance in Latin America. García declared that his country would not pay more than 10 percent of its export receipts in debt service and unilaterally decreed a rollover of debt principal. As of October 1986 Peru had paid only $17.8 million to banks since García became president and was $639 million in arrears on interest payments. The IMF is formally out of the picture, but the World Bank and other official creditors have continued to support Peru. Peru's negotiators claim that they have not suffered as a consequence of this action— commercial loans already having ceased in any case—but acknowledge that lack of export financing may become a problem.[5]

These efforts by Mexico and Peru have encouraged other debtors to seek better terms. From mid-1986 Argentina and Brazil have been engaging in intensive discussions to coordinate trade and debt strategies and since September have pushed Mexico to join them. The demonstration effect has spread even beyond Latin America. In November 1986 the Philippines tried to get its creditors to agree to a twenty-year maturity like Mexico's. Zaire has recently followed the example of Peru in unilaterally declaring it will pay debt service equal to 10 percent of its exports and no more.[6]

Terms and conditions of the rescheduling arrangements are slowly changing, but cooperation among debtors, bankers, and public officials continues. Although feared and resisted by bankers, the linkage of loans to commodity prices (and other concessions) may become inevitable if the system is to remain stable.

The U.S. government is the linchpin of the system. It alone can push banks into making additional concessions as needed and play a mediating role in bank-debtor negotiations. In spite of proclamations to the contrary, sharing costs in the debt crisis is not a simple financial matter but a highly political problem. We are not so

[5]*Latin American Weekly Report*, 9 October 1986.

[6]*Mexico City News*, 17 November 1986.

bold as to expect that the U.S. government can introduce measures which are seen as "bailing out" the banks or debtor countries without some political costs. Cooperation is not painless; it requires mutual adjustment. This fact must be widely understood before any rash moves are made. Yet we believe that these costs pale beside the political and economic costs of intensified discord.

The crisis is manageable. Although the system is resilient, it does not follow that there is a unique and stable distribution of costs. Moving from one distribution to another is not painless: there will always be winners and losers. By taking actions to facilitate bank provisioning against losses, capitalization of interest, and better treatment for debtors, the U.S. government can ease the pain.

APPENDIXES

CHRONOLOGIES OF DEBT RESCHEDULING NEGOTIATIONS

1. ARGENTINA, 1982-86
2. BRAZIL, 1982-86
3. MEXICO, 1982-86
4. POLAND, 1979-86

attractive. Recently these two countries have intensified their trade and other economic links and are making significant overtures to Mexico.

Other debtors have also announced that their breaking point has been reached. Since President García took office in July 1985, Peru has taken the most radical renegotiation stance in Latin America. García declared that his country would not pay more than 10 percent of its export receipts in debt service and unilaterally decreed a rollover of debt principal. As of October 1986 Peru had paid only $17.8 million to banks since García became president and was $639 million in arrears on interest payments. The IMF is formally out of the picture, but the World Bank and other official creditors have continued to support Peru. Peru's negotiators claim that they have not suffered as a consequence of this action— commercial loans already having ceased in any case—but acknowledge that lack of export financing may become a problem.[5]

These efforts by Mexico and Peru have encouraged other debtors to seek better terms. From mid-1986 Argentina and Brazil have been engaging in intensive discussions to coordinate trade and debt strategies and since September have pushed Mexico to join them. The demonstration effect has spread even beyond Latin America. In November 1986 the Philippines tried to get its creditors to agree to a twenty-year maturity like Mexico's. Zaire has recently followed the example of Peru in unilaterally declaring it will pay debt service equal to 10 percent of its exports and no more.[6]

Terms and conditions of the rescheduling arrangements are slowly changing, but cooperation among debtors, bankers, and public officials continues. Although feared and resisted by bankers, the linkage of loans to commodity prices (and other concessions) may become inevitable if the system is to remain stable.

The U.S. government is the linchpin of the system. It alone can push banks into making additional concessions as needed and play a mediating role in bank-debtor negotiations. In spite of proclamations to the contrary, sharing costs in the debt crisis is not a simple financial matter but a highly political problem. We are not so

[5]*Latin American Weekly Report*, 9 October 1986.

[6]*Mexico City News*, 17 November 1986.

Appendix 1

CHRONOLOGY OF DEBT RESCHEDULING NEGOTIATIONS: ARGENTINA, 1982-86

1982

September — Argentina wants to reschedule payments on $15 billion of debt due in the next four months, but bankers are waiting for the United Kingdom to release $1.45 billion in frozen assets.

October — Argentina wants a short-term loan for $1 billion, but bankers are waiting for an IMF agreement.

28 October — IMF gives provisional approval for a $1.5 billion loan. (Banks must contribute $1.5 billion.)

December — IMF requests that 325 lending banks reschedule $5.5 billion of Argentina's debt falling due in 1983, provide a one-year bridge facility of $1.1 billion (the BIS, the usual source of bridge loans, has offered Argentina $750 million secured against the country's gold reserves), and provide a $1.5 billion five-year loan.

31 December — Argentina signs a $1.1 billion short-term loan with an eleven-bank committee.

1983

25 January — IMF agrees to lend Argentina $2.18 billion.

28 January — BIS grants a $500 million short-term loan.

May — Argentina misses May interest payments.

August — $1.5 billion commercial bank loan held up as U.K. bankers protest curbs on moving their funds in Argentina.

15 August — IMF announces that Argentina is complying with its program and commercial loan now goes through.

September — Argentina misses $500 million in mid-September payments.

13 October — First part of the $1.5 billion loan is postponed.

17 October — Argentina asks for delay of installment on $1.1 billion short-term credit.

27 October — Bankers postpone $500 million payment (of $1.5 billion loan) because Argentina failed to pay all interest due by 30 September 1983 ($100 million).

31 October	Eleven-bank committee extends deadline to 30 November 1983 for creditor banks to come up with $500 million loan.
31 October	Civilian government takes over with Raúl Alfonsín as president.

1984

12 January	Argentina and IMF begin negotiations on a new $1.5 billion loan.
6 March	Argentina formally cancels $1.6 billion IMF loan due to expire in April—drew only $700 million. Asks for a new loan. Payments are $2.7 billion overdue now.
29 March	U.S. Treasury proposes short-term rescue loan.
30 March	Plan worked out to keep Argentina current through January 1984. Mexico, Brazil, Colombia, and Venezuela put up $300 million, banks $100 million. United States will pay back countries when Argentina and IMF reach agreement.
18 April	Eleven-bank negotiating committee recommends that Argentina be given until 15 June 1984 to pay back the $750 million due on the December 1982 bridge loan.
30 April	United States extends its $300 million offer by one month.
11 June	Argentina releases its proposed letter of intent to IMF.
15 June	Argentina misses deadline again; United States refuses to extend time limit.
20 June	Argentina pays banks $100 million in back interest.
29 June	Argentina reaches an agreement with the banks as the committee lends it $125 million (guaranteed by Argentine deposits at the Fed) at 1.8 percent over London Inter-Bank Offer Rate (LIBOR); due 15 August 1984 unless Argentina signs with IMF. In that case, deadline will be extended to 1 October 1984. Committee also recommends extending deadline for $750 million that is due until 15 September 1984.
26 July	Argentina repays $50 million to Colombia and announces that it will repay the other Latin American countries by 31 August 1984.
15 August	Argentina repays the $125 million it owes with money it has at the Fed, after bankers refuse to renew the loan.
15 September	Argentina's key creditors agree to extend deadline for $750 million (of a $1.1 billion bridge loan provided in December 1982) on a day-to-day basis.
25 September	Argentina reaches agreement with IMF providing $1.6 billion in new loans.

3 December   Agreement in principle on rescheduling principal due from 1982-85 and private nonguaranteed debt. New credits also extended. (See terms in Table A-1 below.) Not signed formally until August 1985.

1985

16 January   Argentina signs a Paris Club accord to reschedule official debt of $2.1 billion.

18 February   Argentine minister of economy and central bank president resign. Inflation estimated at yearly rate over 1,000 percent.

March   IMF begins review of Argentina's compliance with economic targets agreed in September 1984 and blocks its credit drawings until July, thereby delaying completion of December 1984 commercial bank package.

16 June   Argentina announces new economic package (Austral Plan) and new agreement with IMF. United States arranges a multi-country short-term loan of $480 million to tide Argentina over until IMF disbursement.

August   Rescheduling agreement signed providing for $4.2 billion in fresh loans.

November   Volcker visits Argentina to arrange for $4.2 billion loan (first loan under Baker Plan).

1986

February   Agreement reached with IMF for $865 million in new funds from IMF and banks.

May   Argentina falls out of compliance with IMF. New negotiations commence to find agreement on new pan.

June   Argentina decides to delay further talks with creditors until after results of Mexico's 1986 negotiations (for which the deadline is September World Bank/IMF meetings), hoping to profit from any new concessions Mexico receives from banks.

10 September Argentina and Brazil mutually dismantle trade barriers on a significant list of manufactured goods (especially capital goods). Argentine finance minister hopes to involve Mexico in increased trade and coordinated debt negotiations as well.

Table A-1

TERMS AND CONDITIONS OF BANK DEBT RESTRUCTURINGS AND BANK FINANCIAL PACKAGES: ARGENTINA, 1978-JUNE 1985

Date of Agreement and Type of Debt Rescheduled	Basis	Amount Provided (Millions of dollars)	Grace Period (In years, unless otherwise noted)	Maturity	Interest Rate (Percent spread over LIBOR/U.S. prime)
Bridge loan (1982)[a]		1,300[c]	7 months	14 months	$1\frac{5}{8}$-$1\frac{1}{2}$
New medium-term loan (1983)	New financing	1,500	3	$4\frac{1}{2}$	$2\frac{1}{4}$-$2\frac{1}{8}$
Agreement in principle with Working Committee (3 December 1984):[b]					
Refinancing of medium- and long-term debt					
Public and publicly guaranteed debt					
Due in 1982 and 1983	100 percent of principal	16,552	3	10	$1\frac{3}{8}$-$1\frac{3}{8}$
Due in 1984 and 1985	100 percent of principal		3	12	$1\frac{3}{8}$-$1\frac{3}{8}$
Private sector nonguaranteed debt			3	10	$1\frac{3}{8}$-$1\frac{3}{8}$
New medium-term loan	New financing	3,700	3	10	$1\frac{5}{8}$-$1\frac{1}{4}$
New trade credit deposit facility		500	--	4	$1\frac{3}{8}$-1
Trade credit maintenance facility	Banks would maintain trade credit at levels of 30 September 1984 (estimate)	1,200	--	--	$1\frac{1}{8}$-$\frac{3}{4}$
Standby money market facility	Banks would make available to the central bank on request any amounts outstanding to foreign branches and agencies of Argentine banks on 30 September 1984	1,400	--	--	$\frac{1}{4}$

Source: IMF, Recent Developments in External Debt Restructuring (Washington D.C., October 1985): 48; Occasional Paper 40.

a. An agreement in principle to reschedule arrears at the end of 1982 and public debt falling due in 1983 was reached in January 1983, but the new government requested a renegotiation of this agreement.

b. The agreement also provided the following: the $750 million outstanding under the 1982 bridge loan would be repaid in early 1985 on the first borrowing under the new loan; Argentina would pay at least $750 million before the end of 1984 to reduce interest arrears on Argentine public-sector indebtedness; interest arrears on public-sector indebtedness would be brought current during the first half of 1985; and foreign exchange would be made available to private-sector borrowers so that interest on Argentine private-sector indebtedness could be brought current during the first half of 1985.

c. The cumulative loan disbursements could never exceed $1.1 billion per annum.

Appendix 2

CHRONOLOGY OF DEBT RESCHEDULING NEGOTIATIONS: BRAZIL, 1982-86

1982

September   Mexico declares a moratorium on principal, leading banks to retrench on their lending to Brazil as well.

October   Brazil announces that no rescheduling is needed.

26 November   Brazil asks for a $2-3 billion commercial loan.

1 December   President Reagan announces a $1.2 billion U.S. Treasury loan to Brazil (arranged in October and disbursed in November but not announced until Reagan's visit to Brazil in December).

December (first week)   U.S. banks make a short-term loan of $600 million.

December (second week)   When Brazil's Banco do Brasil cannot balance its books in New York at end of day, big New York banks meet its shortfall (estimated between $50 million and $300 million).

20 December   Central bank president Langoni presents first part of loan program request (Phase I) to banks.

23 December   BIS grants Brazil a $1.2 billion bridge loan (not repaid until end of 1983).

30 December   Brazil stops principal payments.

1983

6 January   Brazil signs IMF letter of intent.

18 February   Brazil asks postponement of $400 million repayment of BIS loan.

25 February   Phase I agreement between banks and Brazil; Brazil receives the following: $4.4 billion in new loans; rescheduling of $4 billion of 1983 debt; maintenance of $8 billion in trade credits; small increase in level of interbank deposits.

February   IMF loans Brazil about $4.9 billion (conditional on Phase I).

3 March   United States announces $400 million bridge loan.

18 April   Banks meet to restore $1.5 billion in interbank lines.

May	IMF suspends its loan. (Brazil did not meet economic targets.) Commercial banks also suspend their loans.
7 October	Phase II negotiated with bank advisory committee.
10 October	Sixty-six creditors agree to tentative terms for Phase II.
22 November	IMF to restart lending, conditional on Phase II. Commercial banks follow IMF lead.
23 November	Western government creditors defer repayment of $3.8 billion due by end of 1984.

1984

27 January	Phase II signed (conditioned on the IMF loan (see terms and conditions in Table A-2 below).
August	Brazil resumes negotiations with banks for multiyear rescheduling agreement.

1985

February	Brazil announces tentative multiyear rescheduling agreement with banks to restructure $45 billion in principal payments due between 1985 and 1991.
14 February	IMF cuts credit to Brazil because Brazil fails to meet austerity targets, thereby jeopardizing multiyear agreement.
4 March	Civilian government takes office. Discussions on how Brazil's economy will be monitored after IMF accord runs out.
10 September	Tentative agreement with banks to reschedule 1985 debt only.
December	No formal agreement reached with IMF; multiyear rescheduling plan scrapped.

1986

28 February	Major de-indexation plan unveiled; heterodox policy followed, not standard IMF plan.
March	Brazil's steering committee of commercial bankers agrees to cut interest rate on one third of outstanding debt.
25 July	Signing ceremony in New York after 80 percent of creditors agree to rescheduling package. Provides rescheduling of 1985 debt over seven years, commencing in 1991; postponement to March 1987 of $9.5 billion in amortization due in 1986; and renewal of $15.5 billion in commercial and interbank lines.

Table A-2

TERMS AND CONDITIONS OF BANK DEBT RESTRUCTURINGS AND BANK FINANCIAL PACKAGES: BRAZIL, 1978-JUNE 1985

Date of Agreement and Type of Debt Rescheduled	Basis	Amount Provided (*Millions of dollars*)	Grace Period (*In years, unless*	Maturity *otherwise noted)*	Interest Rate (*Percent spread over LIBOR/U.S. prime)*
Agreement of 25 February 1983:					
Rescheduling of					
Medium- and long-term debt due in 1983	100 percent of principal	4,532	$2^1/_2$ [a]	8	$2^1/_8$-$1^7/_8$ [c] $2^1/_4$-2
Short-term debt (1983; trade related)	100 percent rollover in 1983	9,800	--	--	. . .
New loan commitments (1983)	New financing	4,400	$2^1/_2$	8	$2^1/_8$-$1^7/_8$ [d]
Agreement of 27 January 1984:					
Rescheduling of					
Medium- and long-term debt due in 1984	100 percent of principal	5,213	5	9	2-$1^3/_4$
Short-term debt (1984; trade related)	100 percent rollover	9,800	--	--	. . .
New loan commitment (1984)	New financing	6,500	5	9	2-$1^3/_4$
Requested by the authorities (December 1984):					
Rescheduling of public- and private-sector debt due in 1985-91	Principal	44,800	Up to 8 [b]	16	$^7/_8$-$1^1/_4$

Source: IMF, *Recent Developments in External Debt Restructuring*, p. 49.

[a] First principal payment due 30 months after rescheduling.

[b] Certain payments are to be made during 1985-93 for amounts falling due during that period.

[c] The spreads over LIBOR/U.S. prime rate are $2^1/_8$ percent/$1^7/_8$ percent for amounts on deposit with the central bank or—as generally acceptable maximums—for loans to public-sector borrowers with official guarantee, Petrobras, and Companhia Vale do Rico Doce (CVRD); $2^1/_4$ percent/2 percent as the generally acceptable maximums for public-sector borrowers without official guarantee, private-sector borrowers with development bank guarantee and for commercial and investment banks under Resolution 63; $2^1/_2$ percent/$2^1/_4$ percent as generally acceptable maximums for private-sector borrowers.

[d] The central bank stands ready to borrow the committed funds at either $2^1/_8$ percent over LIBOR or $1^7/_8$ percent over U.S. prime rate. For loans to other borrowers, the spreads agreed must be acceptable to the central bank, which indicated the following maximums for spreads over LIBOR to be generally acceptable (spreads over U.S. prime rate in parentheses): public-sector borrowers with official guarantee as well as Petrobras and CVRD—$2^1/_8$ percent ($1^7/_8$ percent); public-sector borrowers without official guarantee, private-sector borrowers with development bank guarantee, and Resolution 63 loans to commercial and investment banks—$2^1/_4$ percent (2 percent); private-sector borrowers, including multinationals—$2^1/_2$ percent ($2^1/_2$ percent). Brazil is also prepared to pay a 0.5 percent commitment fee on undisbursed commitments, payable quarterly in arrears, and a 1.5 percent flat facility fee on amounts disbursed, payable at the time of disbursement.

CHRONOLOGY OF DEBT RESCHEDULING NEGOTIATIONS:
MEXICO, 1982-86

1982

July $2.5 billion credit with seventy-five commercial banks signed.

August   Mexico's cash shortage becomes news.

13-22 August   Mexican finance minister Jesús Silva Herzog meets with U.S. Treasury and Fed officials to work out deal in which United States would purchase $1 billion of Mexican oil at discount; Fed would urge BIS to lend $1.85 billion, of which Fed would put up half; and $1 billion would be loaned by Commodity Credit Corporation.

20 August   Silva Herzog meets with bankers at the New York Fed to request a three-month moratorium; bankers agree.

1 September   Mexico nationalizes its banks and imposes exchange controls.

23 November   Moratorium extended to 120 days.

8 December   Mexico reaches a tentative $3.92 billion agreement with IMF, conditional upon banks granting it $5 billion in new credits.

1983

24 February   Draft agreement for banks to lend Mexico $5 billion accepted. Meanwhile, Mexico receives $433 million bridge loan from BIS. First bank disbursement in March.

27 August $5 billion agreement with banks officially signed; $18.8 billion rescheduled.

19 December   Mexico to receive $3.8 in new loans on lenient terms (1 percent below previous loan). Loan officially signed in April 1984.

1984

31 March   Mexico lends $100 million to Argentina; previously had lent Costa Rica $50 million.

8 September   Mexico reaches agreement in principle with thirteen-bank advisory committee. It provides the following: a currency conversion clause; postponement of $20 billion in principal due between

1985 and 1990; softening by banks of previous restructuring pacts for sum of $23.6 billion; improvement of bank terms on $5 billion in loans made in 1983.

1985

31 March   Mexico agrees to sterner measures under third year of IMF austerity plan signed in 1982.

September   Mexico City earthquake; oil prices continue to fall.

1 October   Major banks agree to postpone $1 billion in loan repayments.

1986

January   Oil prices begin to drop precipitously.

February–   Discussions continue on and off on loan and aid package to
July   Mexico.

May   Under pressure from the U.S. government and IMF, Mexico petitions to join GATT.

July   Mexico joins GATT under conditions significantly less favorable than those it negotiated, and then rejected, in late 1979.

             Agreement reached with IMF, contingent upon later acceptance by banks, which promises significant innovations favorable to Mexico—notably linkage of loan conditions to international oil prices and domestic economic growth. Mexico also seeks non-market interest and maturity concessions from private creditors.

September   One week before deadline of annual World Bank/IMF meeting, banks reach agreement with Mexico. As compared to previous packages, the accord is extremely favorable: $12 billion in new loans, half from banks, half from official sources; spread of less than one percent over LIBOR; previously rescheduled debt of $43.7 billion (out of total debt of $96 billion up to this package) is given a new, longer grace period (seven years) and maturity (twenty years); contingency facility of $1.7 billion provided by commercial banks, of which the majority is to be dispensed only under IMF discretion. Facility is linked to Mexican domestic economic growth and to external shocks.

Table A-3

TERMS AND CONDITIONS OF BANK DEBT RESTRUCTURINGS AND BANK FINANCIAL PACKAGES: MEXICO: 1978-JUNE 1985

Date of Agreement and Type of Debt Rescheduled	Basis	Amount Provided (Millions of dollars)	Grace Period (In years, unless otherwise noted)	Maturity	Interest Rate (Percent spread over LIBOR/U.S. prime)
Agreement of 27 August 1983:[a]					
Rescheduling of public-sector short-, medium-, and long-term debt due 23 August 1982-31 December 1984[b]					
Syndicated loan[c]	100 percent of principal	18,800	4	8	1-7/8-1-3/4
	New financing (net)	5,000	3	6	2-1/4-2-1/8
Settlement of interest in arrears on private sector's debt[d]	–	1,367	–	–	1-7/8
Agreement of April 1984:					
New loan	New financing	3,800	5-1/2	10	1-1/2-1-1/8
Agreement in principle of 8 September 1984:					
Rescheduling of public medium- and long-term debt not previously rescheduled, falling due from 1985 to 1990	100 percent of principal	20,100	1	14[f]	{ 7/8 in 1985-86; 1-1/8 in 1987-91; 1-1/4 in 1992-98 }
Rescheduling of public medium- and long-term debt previously rescheduled					
Due in 1987	100 percent of principal	5,800	--	14[f]	{ 7/8 in 1985-86; 1-1/8 in 1987-91; 1-1/4 in 1992-98 }
Due from 1988 to 1990	100 percent of principal	17,800	--	14[f]	
Rescheduling of 1983 syndicated loan[e]		5,000	5	10	1-1/2-1-1/8

Source: IMF, *Recent Developments in External Debt Restructuring,* p. 54.

[a] Agreement took effect with disbursement of a new loan in March 1983.

[b] For the purpose of the rescheduling, Mexico's public-sector debt (short-, medium-, and long-term) excludes the following: loans made, guaranteed, insured, or subsidized by official agencies in the creditor countries; publicly issued bonds, private placements (including Japanese yen-denominated registered private placements), and floating rate certificates of deposit and notes (including floating rate notes); debt to official multilateral entities; forward exchange and precious metal contracts; spot and lease obligations in respect of movable property; short-term import- and export-related trade credits; interbank obligations (including placements) of the foreign agencies and branches of Mexican banks, excluding guarantees on interbank placements; financing secured by legally recognized security interest in ships, aircraft, and drilling rigs; and the central bank's obligations arising from the arrangements to liquidate interest payments in arrears.

[c] The $5 billion loan was raised in the form of a medium-term international syndicated credit in which banks participated on the basis of their pro rata exposure to Mexico as of 23 August 1982. The loan document included a specific reference to a written explanation and confirmation from the IMF managing director with respect to $2-2.5 billion in financial assistance to be obtained from official creditors (other than the IMF), a requirement to provide information about the implementation of the financial program, a request on the part of the lending syndicate not to object to the final restructuring principles of the contemplated rescheduling operation, the customary cross-default clause, a specification of events of defaults (including the failure of Mexico to comply with the performance criteria agreed with the IMF in connection with the three-year extended arrangement, and nonmembership), and the implementation of the proposed mechanism to eliminate the interest arrears on the private-sector debt. In addition, interbank exposure was restored and would be maintained through the end of 1986 at $5.2 billion.

[d] Specifically, Mexican private borrowers owing interest on foreign bank debts payable in foreign currency and outstanding prior to 1 September 1982 could use the procedures proposed by the Mexican authorities to settle interest payments due in the period from 1 August 1982 to 31 January 1983. Settlement had to be made by depositing the local currency equivalent of the amount of interest due in foreign currency, at the controlled exchange rate of the date at which the deposit was constituted. Special foreign currency deposits were being opened by the foreign lenders with the Bank of Mexico, and the amounts of interest owed were being credited to these accounts. Ten percent of the outstanding balance in these accounts was paid to creditors on 31 January 1983, while the remainder had to be settled subject to the availability of foreign exchange. As of 7 March 1984, all outstanding arrears were eliminated.

[e] $250 million of the 1983 syndicated loan was prepaid in 1985.

[f] There are no rescheduling fees, and under certain conditions banks are allowed to switch their loans from dollars to home country currencies. Rescheduling of previously rescheduled debt falling due from 1987 to 1990 is conditional upon the achievement of Mexico's own economic targets to be monitored on the basis of enhanced Article IV consultations with the IMF beginning in 1986. Maturities shown relate to the date of the agreement in principle.

Appendix 4

CHRONOLOGY OF DEBT RESCHEDULING NEGOTIATIONS:
POLAND, 1979-86

1979

January   Bank Handlowy (Polish central bank) raises $550 million from consortium of Western banks.

1980

April   Thirty-two banks meet to discuss possibility of raising "substantial loan" for Poland. Only $300 million is raised for seven years at 1.5 percent above LIBOR.

June   Poland needs new loan to service its $26 billion debt.

October   Soviet Union grants Poland $1.1 billion loan, making the total $2.5 billion for 1980.

1981

February   Soviet Union reschedules four years of Polish debt.

31 March   Bank Handlowy tells Western creditors it needs time to pay the $2.4 billion due in 1981. Twenty-bank working group to negotiate for 501 bank creditors. Poland to reschedule $2.4 billion to banks and $2.4 billion to official creditors.

April   Western governments assemble "huge injection of food aid" for Poland.

20 April   Paris Club agrees to reschedule $2.4 billion in principal and interest for 1981.

1 May   Bank working group rejects Polish demand for renegotiating commercial debt on same terms as Paris Club agreement.

20 May   Bank working group suggests rescheduling terms for $2.4 billion due in 1981. (See terms agreed to in Table A-4 below.)

September   Banks threaten to declare Poland in default if agreement is not signed.

1 October   A task force agrees to reschedule 95 percent of debt due between 26 March and 1 December 1981. The terms: seven years;

69

four-year grace period; interest: 1.75 percent above LIBOR; 1 percent rescheduling fee.

10 November	Poland formally applies to rejoin IMF. (It had been a founding member but had dropped out in 1950.)
December	Rescheduling agreement suspended pending Polish payment of all 1981 interest.
13 December	Martial law imposed.

1982

11 January	NATO members refuse to reschedule official loans until martial law is lifted and Polish government opens dialogue with church and Solidarity trade union.
31 January	U.S. administration repays $71 million that Poland owed to U.S. banks under Commodity Credit Corporation but does not require banks to declare Poland in default.
8 February	Senator Daniel Moynihan introduces legislation in U.S. Senate to declare Poland in default (not passed).
16 March	Poland repays all overdue 1981 interest.
6 April	Agreement to reschedule Poland's 1981 commercial debt ($2.4 billion) is signed.
July	Negotiations on 1982 debt rescheduling begin.
3 November	Agreement to reschedule 1982 commercial debt is signed. The terms: interest: 1.75 percent over LIBOR; 5 percent of $2.4 billion in principal due, rescheduled for 7.5 years, to be repaid in seven semiannual installments; four-year grace period; remaining 5 percent is repayable in two installments on 20 August and 20 November 1983; 50 percent of the $1.1 billion due in 1982 will be recycled as three-year trade credits.; the other half of the interest will be repaid in three installments on 19 November 1982, 20 December 1982, and 20 March 1983.

1983

13 June	Poland proposes that commercial banks reschedule all remaining debts over twenty years, but idea is rejected.
22 July	Martial law lifted.
August	Western governments agree in principle to resume rescheduling talks.
18 August	Poland and its international bank creditors sign memorandum of understanding to reschedule Poland's 1983 debt.

2 November   President Reagan formally agrees to renegotiate part of Poland's official debt.

3 November   Poland signs 1983 rescheduling agreement with commercial banks. The terms: $1.5 billion in principal spread over ten years with five years' grace; interest to be repaid in three installments by end of 1983, but 65 percent of that to be immediately recycled through short-term trade credits.

1984

28 April   Eighteen-member negotiating team representing more than 500 Western banks agrees to reschedule $1.615 billion due by end of 1987. Agreement is due to be formally signed in July.

1985

July   Poland reschedules $11 billion official 1982-84 debt.

20 November   Official debt due in 1985 rescheduled ($1.3 billion).

1986

June   Poland re-reschedules commercial $2.06 billion debt due in 1986 and 1987 at $1^{3}/_{8}$ percent over LIBOR. (Total debt stands at about $31 billion.) Poland also becomes member of IMF, an action which had been blocked by an American veto until President Reagan decided to lift veto in early 1985. Poland's hope is that IMF membership will result in increases in future multilateral and bank credits.

Table A-4

TERMS AND CONDITIONS OF BANK DEBT RESTRUCTURINGS AND BANK FINANCIAL PACKAGES:
POLAND, 1978-JUNE 1985

Date of Agreement and Type of Debt Rescheduled	Basis	Amount Provided (Millions of dollars)	Grace Period (In years, unless otherwise noted)	Maturity	Interest Rate (Percent spread over LIBOR/U.S. prime)
Agreement of April 1982:[a]					
Medium-term debt due 26 March 1981-December 1981	95 percent of principal	2,300	4	7	1¾
Agreement of November 1982:[b]					
Medium-term debt due in 1982, including arrears on unrescheduled maturities due in 1981	95 percent of principal	2,300	4	7½	1¾-1½
Agreement of November 1983:[c]					
Medium-term debt due during 1983	95 percent of principal	1,400	5	10	1⅞
Agreement of 28 April 1984:					
Medium- and long-term debt due in 1984-87	95 percent of principal	1,615	5	10	1¾
New trade credits[d]	New financing	235	–	5	1⅝
Rollover of short-term credit facility[d]	. . .	465	. . .	. . .	. . .

Source: IMF, *Recent Developments in External Debt Restructuring*, p. 62.

[a]The agreement, which covers maturities due during 26 March-31 December 1981, was effective 10 May 1982. Short-term facilities and interbank deposits were specifically excluded.

[b]A six-month trade credit, revolving up to three years, was extended under separate agreement; the amount of the credit was equivalent to 50 percent of the $1.1 billion in interest due.

[c]A six-month trade credit, revolving up to three years, was extended under separate agreement.

[d]In 1985 the short-term credit facility was rolled over, and further trade credits, revolving every six months for up to 4-5 years, are to be extended

VINOD K. AGGARWAL is Assistant Professor of Political Science at the University of California, Berkeley. From 1984 to 1986 he held a Rockefeller International Relations Fellowship, and he was a Guest Scholar at the Brookings Institution in 1984-1985. He is the author of *Liberal Protectionism: The International Politics of Organized Textile Trade* (1985) and several articles on the politics of trade and finance.

INSTITUTE OF INTERNATIONAL STUDIES
UNIVERSITY OF CALIFORNIA, BERKELEY

215 Moses Hall   Berkeley, California 94720

CARL G. ROSBERG, *Director*

Monographs published by the Institute include:

RESEARCH SERIES

LIST OF PUBLICATIONS *(continued)*

POLICY PAPERS IN INTERNATIONAL AFFAIRS